SEPECAT JAGUAR

Previous page: Posing neatly for the camera aircraft, a single-seater of No 17 Squadron RAF shows off the tail warning radar installation which intersects its fin. *Image in Industry*

Above: S4, the first Jaguar for the RAF, takes off from Warton at the start of its delivery flight to Lossiemouth. *BAe*

Modern Combat Aircraft 14

SEPECAT JAGUAR

Arthur Reed

LONDON
IAN ALLAN LTD

Acknowledgements

The author wishes to thank the many people in the British and French aircraft industries who found time to talk to him on the subject of Jaguar, and in particular Trevor Tarr, of British Aerospace, Warton, whose constant help and unlimited enthusiasm gave this book its essential re-heat on take-off.

Front Cover: Jaguar GR1 of No 41 Squadron landing at Bardufoss AB, Norway, during the NATO Exercise 'Alloy Express 82' in March 1982; the aircraft was finished in a temporary camouflage scheme for winter operations during deployment in North Norway. *Denis J. Calvert*

First published 1982

ISBN 0 7110 1215 6

Published by Ian Allan Ltd, Shepperton, Surrey; and printed by Ian Allan Printing Ltd at their works at Coombelands in Runnymede, England

Contents

1 Killing Old Concepts 5

2 Cross-Channel Accord 18

3 Prototypes, Prototypes 24

4 Green Light from France 33

5 Deciding the Shape 41

6 All Singing, All Dancing 46

7 Into French Service 58

8 A High Performance Little Ship 73

9 Selling Jaguar Abroad 91

10 'Now Try to Stop it! 101

Appendix: Jaguar Attrition 110

1 Killing Old Concepts

The development as a joint project between Britain and France of the Jaguar low-level strike aircraft must be seen as a watershed in the history of military aviation, in that it was the first to break away from the old air-superiority fighter concept. It was designed specifically to operate in the northern Europe theatre, and it was also designed specifically to be compatible with up-to-date warfare philosophies. Its developers had to overcome a faction within the Royal Air Force which was suspicious and even downright hostile towards the concept. The faction contained officers who, at the time that the concept was being developed, in the early 1960s, had achieved middle and senior rank, but whose minds were still wedded to doing 'upward Charlies' at 45,000ft, and who would have been very happy indeed with a project on the lines of the F-16 from the United States, often referred to as 'the modern Spitfire'.

Theirs was the 'fighter jockey' mentality, and a great deal of credit has to go to the RAF Air Staff and the operational requirement people in the Ministry of Defence of that time that they were able to break away from that point of view and specify a little aeroplane in which operational priorities were realigned, and which could hardly have been more different from the 'ground attack fighters' which had been developed hitherto. Jaguar was designed to operate at low level, with the sophisticated defensive environment of Europe in mind, and with a very accurate attack system, the philosophy being that it was no use flying sorties against targets if you cannot find the target, and that it was no use finding targets, but then being unable to hit them on the nose. A lot of development went into the low-level and bad-weather navigation system and into extremely accurate weapon aiming, using computers. Some of these were developments of systems designed for the TSR2 bomber, cancelled in April, 1965.

The new concept which went into the attack version of the Jaguar has led directly to the Tornado. The threat was recognised at the time of the Jaguar development as being that of the Russians, with their huge preponderance of troops, armour and guns, rolling into western Europe; it was seen that in the face of such an advance there would not be time for a traditional air-superiority battle to decide who is controlling the air space, and that it was necessary to hit them, with something like the Jaguar, and latterly the Tornado, right at the beginning (this realistic attitude was summed up in the early 1960s by a story that had two Russian officers standing in the Travellers' Club in Paris watching their troops holding a victory parade down the Champs Elysee; 'Well', says one, 'it is a great day for the motherland; it has

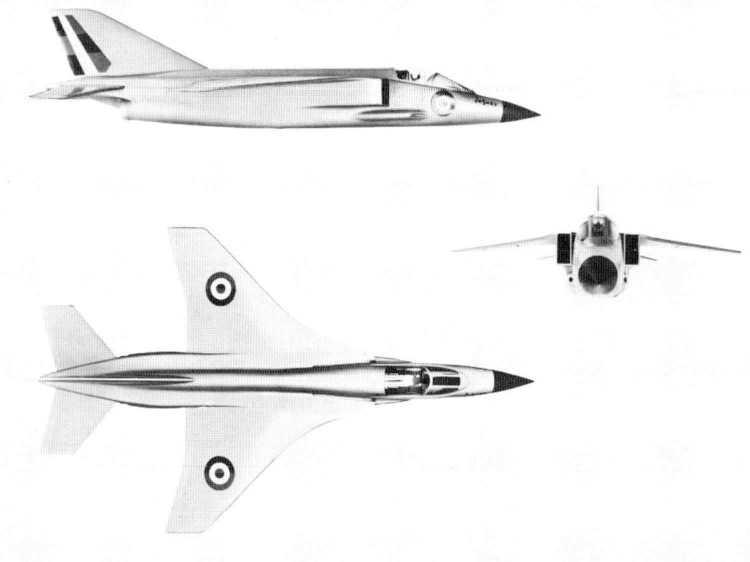

Left: This 1966 artist's impression of what was to become Jaguar shows very different lines to those of the aircraft which is in service today. *The Times*

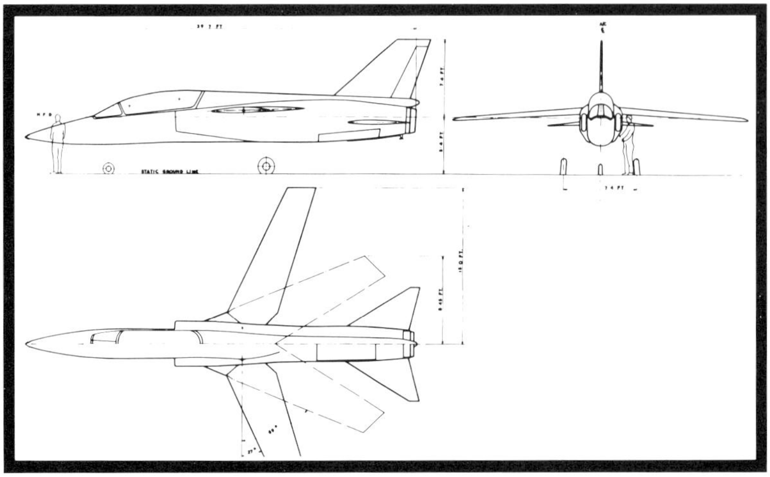

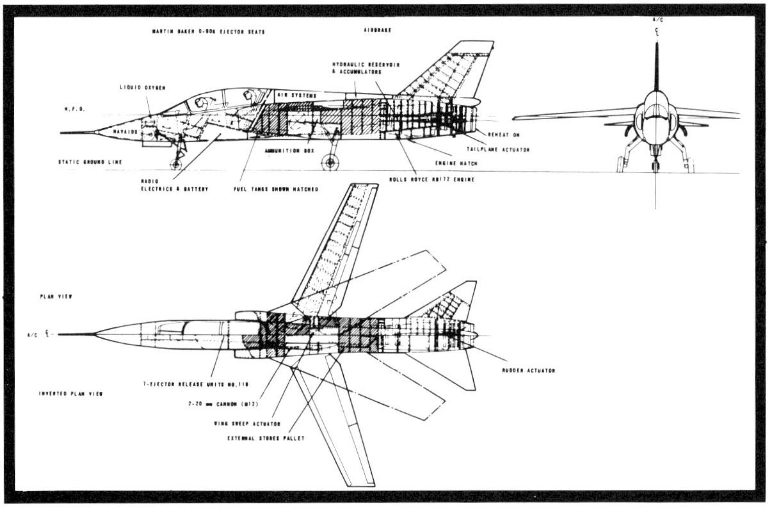

Right: Rare general arrangement drawings of what was to be 'son of Jaguar', the AA-107, with one Adour and variable geometry wing. BAC planned to develop it with the Australians, but no funding was forthcoming from the British Government. *BAe*

been a great victory. Pity we lost the air superiority battle').

The French version of the Jaguar went by no means as far down the road as that taken by the RAF, having less sophisticated, and therefore cheaper, avionics. Jeffrey Quill, who was seconded from British Aircraft Corporation to be sales director for SEPECAT, the joint Anglo-French Jaguar company, recalled how the concept was conceived. He said:

'In Britain the need for a replacement for the Gnat was brewing up. The idea of international collaborations in aerospace was very popular. There was a lot of thought about the Gnat replacement going on up at BAC Warton, and the idea emerged that the new trainer would be a supersonic aeroplane, Mach 1.2-1.3. Over in France, and simultaneously, there was another requirement called the ECAT for a small operational trainer with an additional role as a light attack aircraft. The ECAT competition in France was won by Breguet, then under General Henri Ziegler, who later took over Airbus Industrie.

'In Britain, you couldn't get a place like Warton drawing lines on bits of paper for a Mach 1.3 two-seat trainer without them closely examining operational roles for it and thinking of hanging weapons on it. At that time, Peter Thorneycroft was Minister of Defence and Messmer was his opposite number in France. They used to go to talk to each other now and again. On one occasion they had breakfast together in Paris. Thorneycroft said that we were trying to put together a replacement for the Gnat, and Messmer said, "We've got the same thing going on over here. So why don't we get together".

'So at that point the two air staffs, with some

reluctance I think, were told to talk to each other and to produce a jointly-agreed requirement which would lead to a joint project. That was how the Jaguar started. The original French requirement was subsonic, in-service 1970, while the British requirement was supersonic, in-service 1974, so that a fair amount of compression went on. The RAF injected into the Jaguar stringent tactical requirements, low-level with a really good navigation system and weapon-aiming system. The French, who wanted cheapness, were much more disposed to write the sort of requirement you might have written around a ground-attack Hunter. Therefore, the British tactical S version came out much superior and sophisticated in its standard of equipment to the French A version.

'Although the airframes of the main S and A versions are similar, the completed aircraft are as different as chalk and cheese in equipment and what they can do. The more ambitious British requirements inevitably began to affect the geometry of the aeroplane and we finished up with a smaller wing than the French would have liked. There is never anything for nothing in aircraft design, and what was sacrificed in this case, and deliberately so, was thrust-to-weight ratio. First of all we wanted low-level range, and there was no way we could put in an engine which would give us a ratio of one-to-one because you would never have got half way down the road.

'When the new Adour, based on the Rolls-Royce RB172, and selected in late 1964, was developed for the Jaguar, the thrust-to-weight ratio was deliberately sacrificed on the knowledge that everybody has, that engines grow in thrust. Everybody said, "Don't worry, Rolls-Royce will squeeze more power out of it". So we had the problem, which the Americans always try to avoid, of developing a new airframe and a new engine. The Adour was, of course, an Anglo-French engine, with Turbomeca as Rolls-Royce's partners (Turbomeca had been developing the Tourmalet engine for the ECAT programme), and when it was working well it was an Anglo-French engine, but as soon as it was working badly, which was mostly, it was a Rolls-Royce engine.

'The engine had to be sized around the cruise condition, rather as those for an airliner are, and thus of moderate dry thrust. It needed very good specific fuel consumption, and hence a high by-pass ratio. At the same time, it had to develop very high thrust for take-off and supersonic operation, and a low-level dash capability. These demands required a high degree of reheat augmentation, and it all had to be contained in a small, short engine.

'The very early engine problems were bad, although no worse than could be expected, but there was never any suggestion that the whole project should be cancelled because of them because it had so much political steam behind it. Jaguar might be said to have coined the now-familiar saying that although joint projects are more difficult to get started, once they get going they are a lot more difficult to cancel. The main initial problems were that the engine was slow in development, it didn't work very well, and there weren't enough of them. There was a point where we had three prototypes which should have had six engines, but we only had three engines, and they were being changed around.

'The early flying programme was thus a bit marginal all the time. But we British used to say, "It's all right, it's Rolls-Royce", and then came the terrible

Below: Jaguar prototypes 01 and 02 are together in this January 1968 picture taken at the Breguet works at Villacoublay. Both were then in the final stages of assembly, and 01 made the maiden flight on 8 September that year. *BAe*

moment in 1971 when we were all over with the French in Villacoublay and we heard that Rolls-Royce had gone bankrupt. The Adours were also expensive, and the French used to tell us that an Atar had twice the power of an Adour, and cost half as much. That may have been so, but the Atar would not have been much good at low level.

'One of the points which the French made when they cancelled the maritime version of the Jaguar was that they were dissatisfied with the single-engine approach to the aircraft carrier, but it has to be remembered that they replaced it with the single-engined Super Etendard, which had been considerably developed from the earlier versions. But they also had their budgetary problems. It suited Dassault to build more Etendards, and it suited the French Ministry of Defence's budget. This was in 1973 after Dassault had merged with Breguet.

'Up to then we had had an excellent relationship with Breguet, and then it began to get more difficult. After Dassault had taken over the French side of Jaguar we used to have marketing meetings with them and say, how come you are trying to sell an F1 or a Mirage 111b against the Jaguar, and they used to say, "What about the Lightning?", and it was in vain that you would point out that the Lightning was out of production.

'It has to be remembered that there was no airborne test-bed programme with the Adour. The engine and the Jaguar airframe took to the air for the first time on the same day, unlike TSR2, and all of the development problems were still in it when it took off. It was not until part-throttle reheat was fitted that these problems started to be ironed out.

Above: The second Jaguar prototype in a test rig at the Breguet works at Villacoublay, near Paris, in early 1968. *The Times*

'I can remember attending the meeting at the Ministry of Defence in London when we were told that agreement had been made with France to design, develop and produce a joint aeroplane. All that existed at that time were the draft national requirements. The agreement had the status of an international treaty and neither side could cancel unilaterally. The effect on industry was immediate. Confidence was created, and designers, development engineers and financial controllers could get down to the business of planning their programmes in the best and most economical manner.

'The benefits of this situation far outweighed the difficulties and problems inherent in the collaborative process. To people who were sometimes tempted to say, "We could do this whole thing much better if we were doing it on our own", one could safely reply, "If you were doing it on your own, old cock (or *mon brave*), you wouldn't be doing it all, and don't you forget it".

'At the MoD meeting, we were told that development and financing would be done on a 50-50 basis. Breguet would be in the position of design leaders on the airframe, and Rolls-Royce would have design leadership on the engine. I can remember walking out of the meeting with Sir George Edwards, then chairman of BAC, and he said, jokingly, "Who are these people Breguet? Somebody had better get over there quickly and make contact with them". The next day I

Above: The 02 prototype is rolled out of its hangar for the first time at the end of April 1968. *The Times*

made contact by telephone with Paul Jaillard, of Breguet, and we then went in a small party to them at Villacoublay. We had an appointment, and we knocked on their door and said, "Hallo, we are from the British Aircraft Corporation, and we understand we're going to design an aeroplane together". They said, "Come in", and it all started from there. The project was meant to be based on the French ECAT design, and the task from that point onwards was to bend and squeeze and stretch the ECAT design until it could meet the joint proposals. It was then decided that we ought to form a joint company which would act as the receiver of contracts from the two governments. This was SEPECAT. We had an excellent relationship with Breguet who were very good people, and an atmosphere of mutual respect soon developed. They were very enthusiastic, because it was really their ECAT fighter, the Breguet 121, and the two governments had already signed for a total of 300 aircraft. This was marvellous news, because normally you just built a prototype or two and then waited for somebody to cancel it. From the outset we had a full programme, and everything could be properly planned. Industry had put up with piecemeal programmes for far too long.

'All went very well, and we all used to go rushing back and forwards between Warton and Villacoublay. The early meetings had all the British ranged along one side of the table and all the French along the other. We had no agreement about the language, although the French were much better at English than we were at French. But everybody started taking courses in French. We developed this Franglais sort of communication, but mostly it was was all done in English.

'In any aircraft company there are fundamental conflicts of interests always going on — the design people and the production people are always ganging up against each other, with the design people asking why the production people don't get themselves into the 20th century, the production people complaining about the designers being unable to make up their minds, and everybody fighting with the commercial people. The job of the top management is to referee it all. After the early days of Breguet-BAC it was very interesting to see that instead of the French adopting attitudes against the British, the Anglo-French design people were ganging up together and the Anglo-French production people were ganging up together and the Anglo-French commercial people were ganging up, and you got an exact repetition of the national situation.

'Under the SEPECAT arrangement there was a director, either French or English, who had the final say-so in case of disagreement in various areas, but this system was hardly ever invoked. It actually became the Jaguar in the week before the Paris show, 1965. We had to find a name that meant the same in both languages. There were about half a dozen names suggested. Charles Gardner, publicity director of BAC, and one or two other people produced a list. The name Etoile was on it, but was hurriedly scratched. We had to get in touch with Joe Lyons, of Jaguar Cars, to get his OK over the telephone. He then went off abroad,

and in his absence, one of his people read in the papers about this new aircraft called the Jaguar. He kicked up a fuss about it, and we had to tell him we had asked the boss.*

'We didn't even know what it looked like at that air show, but we had a wooden model of the Breguet 121. Two years later we had a wooden mock-up of the Jaguar. The 1967 Paris show was the one when it rained heavily. The mock-up began to droop, and a Breguet man was seen underneath it drilling holes in the wings to let the water out.

'For us it was disastrous when, in the course of a rationalisation of the French aircraft industry, Breguet were taken over by Dassault (although technically the take-over was the other way round) in June, 1967, the full merger happening in 1971. M. Dassault had been infuriated when Breguet received the ECAT contract over his own design, and by the time of the takeover he had all sorts of prototypes flying around or on the drawing board, the F1, the F2 the G4 and the G8, variable geometry and otherwise. By this time the production order had been increased to 400 Jaguars from the original 300. Dassault was not going to argue about that, because it meant money coming in, but the last thing that he wanted was that this little aeroplane, the philosophy of which he did not agree with, spilling over into the export market, where he was having a fine old time selling Mirages.

*Charles Gardner, in his history *British Aircraft Corporation* (published 1981 by Batsford) says the name was suggested by Ziegler and was settled by one telephone call. Neither air force was consulted, 'a process which can take literally years'.

'It is fair to say that every Jaguar that has been sold abroad, whether in South America, the Middle East, or India, has been sold against the implacable opposition of Dassault, backed by the powerful French defence sales organisations. In India we had no American rival, but this was a great fight, which we won, against the French — our partners, who were trying to sell the F1. It was made more difficult by the fact that you could not put in a detailed submission without Dassault knowing a lot about it, because they were going to have to build half of it. So they knew most of the time what we were doing.

'We originally started off with the idea that SEPECAT would act as main contractors for Jaguar in the export market, but it became apparent that there was no machinery to make this work. It then became either a British or a French main contract. In the case of the British, BAC would sign a contract with a foreign customer and Dassault would fall into line as the principal sub-contractor, and if the French had sold Jaguar we should have become the sub-contractor. We should have sold more if it had not been for this French intransigence, but you have to remember that the sales record of the Jaguar is not bad, and it is also a fact that the aircraft, designed as it was for the northern Europe theatre of operations, does not suit everybody. Only countries which have fought a war, such as Israel and India, really understood its philosophy — in the case of India, where there is usually a dust haze, the scenery was littered with bits of Hunters and Gnats and Soviet-built Su-7s which had failed to find their targets, or to find their way back to base.

Left: With part of its rear opened up to allow access, a Jaguar runs up its Adours in October 1969 when the manufacturers were trying to establish time between overhauls of 1,000 hours. *BAe*

Right: Two French ground crew contemplate an early Jaguar as it runs up its engines. This prototype had original design features which were quickly changed — solid, rather than perforated air brakes, splitter plates in the engine intakes, and a short front undercarriage door. *Image in Industry*

Below: Rear view of E01 running up in France was intended to demonstrate the aircraft's ease of engine maintainability. *BAe*

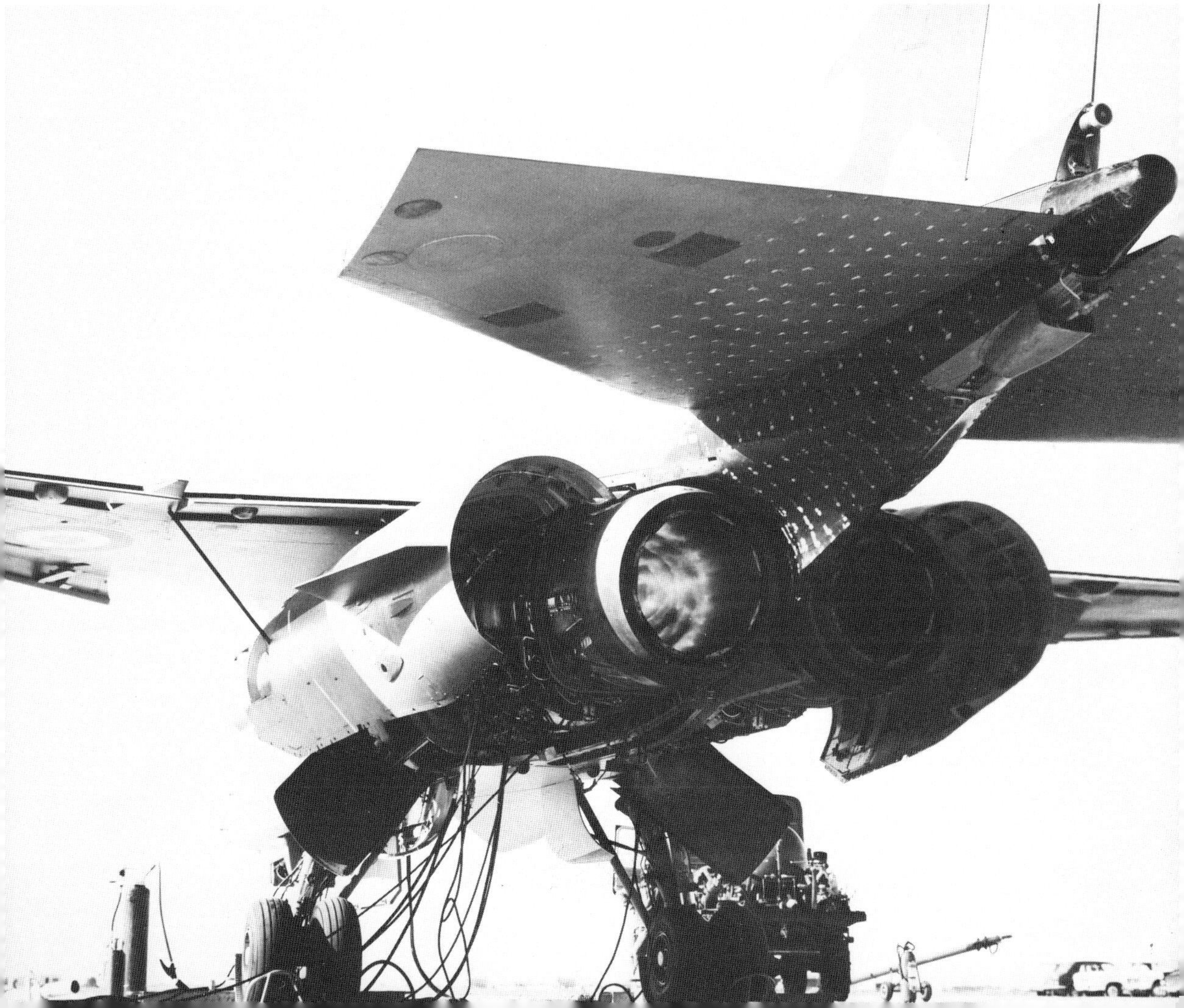

'The sale that took the longest was the Indian one. It was in 1966 that we started, and although our aircraft was selected in 1973, it was 1978 when the deal finally went through. It is an interesting reflection on the business of military aircraft sales in general, that I took the first Anglo-French sales team to India in 1966 to give Jaguar presentations to the IAF Air Staff, to the Defence Ministry, and to Hindustan Aircraft Ltd, in order to suggest that they should commence long-term planning to produce Jaguars at Bangalore, as it was a natural and logical successor to the Gnat.

'It was 12 years, and many, many visits later that the contract was finally signed. This order was won in the face of bitter competition from France. Wg Cdr A. R. Keys, who was a member of the Jaguar project office at Warton under Ivan Yates, accompanied me on most of my visits to India and made a major contribution towards selling the operational concepts of Jaguar to the Indian Air Staff. He is now in charge of the British Aerospace Jaguar office in India.

'Later, when it became a matter of contract negotiations, which were far-reaching and complex, the late Peter Grocock, and Dick Evans, who is now commercial director of BAe, Warton, played major roles, while Sir Frederick Page gave maximum support throughout. There were times during the 12-year Indian sales campaign when all seemed lost, and the economic, financial and political difficulties insurmountable. The Indian sale is a prime example of the most important motto for aircraft salesmen, "Never give up".'

Jeffrey Quill enumerated over 30 other countries where he and teams from BAC tried to sell Jaguar. The shortest deal was in Oman — wrapped up in three months. Belgium nearly joined the programme in about 1967 on the basis of 100 aircraft, but in the end bought Mirage 5s. There was also a possibility that West Germany might have joined, but they hung on for Tornado. Switzerland looked at it, together with eight other types of aircraft; BAC even designed a collapsible tail fin so that the aircraft would fit into the Swiss underground hangars.

There was a big sales effort in Japan, but the Japanese decided to develop their own aircraft, which looks remarkably like Jaguar, and which also has the Adour engine. In 1969, the team went all round South America, and there were hopes that the M (maritime) version might be sold to Brazil and the Argentine. As a result of a sales tour of Australia and New Zealand, 'son of Jaguar' — the AA107 — emerged in late 1968, a trainer with one Adour with reheat and a variable-sweep wing, which would have had a, 'most spectacular' performance. It was designed jointly by BAC and Australian teams, but it collapsed because the British Government would not put up development

Left: A jubilant and significant moment in the Jaguar story. Bernard Witt, Breguet test pilot, is congratulated after the first flight at Istres, France, on 8 September 1968 by (left to right) Ivan Yates, Freddie Page, G. Ricard and B. Vallieres. *BAe*

Right: Bernard Witt, in the cockpit, on first flight day, 8 September 1968 *BAe*

money — on the grounds that it had already got the Jaguar.

Jaguar International emerged when more thrust was needed for the export market, and Rolls-Royce produced the dash 26 version of the Adour. This made it a proposition to introduce air-to-air combat for the Jaguar and to fit Sidewinders. Warton, as a private venture, introduced over-wing pylons, because there was not any room left underneath. This was a purely British development. Jaguar International covered everything which was not destined for the British or French air forces and was, 'all things to all customers'.

Between 1973 and 1975, BAC tried desperately hard to sell Jaguar International to the four-nation consortium, Belgium, the Netherlands, Norway and Denmark which had been formed to find a common solution to their need to replace their Starfighters, and other ageing types, while giving them all economic and industrial advantages. France was promoting the F1, Sweden the Viggen and America the F-16, the latter entry raising the fundamental question of whether such a large European re-equipment programme should be fulfilled by yet another dollar purchase from the US. Jeffrey Quill:

'We decided that Jaguar should be brought into the competition, but by no stretch of the imagination could we market it in the fighter role. However, as the Starfighter was in service in the attack role as well as the air-defence role, and as Jaguar was vastly superior to the F1 and the F-16 in the attack role, we proposed a two-type solution. This was, that Jaguar should re-equip the attack squadrons, and the F1 should re-equip the interceptor squadrons.

'There was a very strong case for the proposal. It was both an international and European solution, so it was good politically. Militarily, it was also excellent. In the attack role, Jaguar was greatly superior to any other aircraft available within the time and price range. In the fighter/interceptor role, the F1 was an excellent aircraft, rivalled only by the Lightning, which was out of production, and the F-16 which, at that time, was neither developed, nor in production.

'The Jaguar was also destined for large-scale service with RAF Germany, a main element in the 2nd Allied Tactical Air Force, of which both the Belgian and Dutch air forces were also part. There was, therefore, great opportunity for commonality of logistic support, inter-operability and operational procedures. The F1 was ordered in quantity for the French Air Force, and was also therefore a going concern in Western Europe. Although it was purely French and not part of NATO, the logistic advantages were obvious. Other advantages were that a comprehensive industrial offset programme could have been built around the two-part solution, while procurement and research and development costs would have been lower.

'This altogether excellent proposal failed for two principal reasons. Dassault refused to cooperate with BAC, in spite of the fact that he had a 50% interest in Jaguar and a 100% interest in the F1. He remained convinced that he was going to get the whole four-nation order for the F1, and was not interested in sharing the cake with anybody. In this attitude, he was supported by the French Government defence sales organisation. In other words, France was too greedy, finished up with nothing, and opened the European market for the F-16, which the four nations eventually bought.

'Secondly, the attitude of the British defence sales organisation in Whitehall was lukewarm almost to the point of hostility. This attitude was puzzling to us, and the reasons for it were never clear. The British ambassadors in both Brussels and The Hague, Sir David Muirhead and Sir John Barnes, together with

SAUVETAGE

their staffs, gave as much support to us as they were reasonably able in face of the hostile attitudes adopted in London.

'With the French refusing to cooperate, and with Whitehall adopting a negative and totally unenterprising stance in the matter, BAC was unable to push this proposal through, although investigations carried out after the F-16 decision had been taken showed that a great deal more impact had been made, especially in Belgium than we dared to hope at the time. Thus, a great opportunity for European aerospace was thrown away, and a vital European market handed on a plate to the US industry.

'It was unfortunate that while all this was going on, the Jaguar was only in the early stages of its operational service in RAF Germany, and had not had time to demonstrate its remarkable capabilities in the attack, interdiction and tactical reconnaissance roles, which it subsequently did by cleaning up all the international NATO tactical competitions, and by making a great impact in the American tactical exercises Red Flag in the Nevada desert.

'It is probably fair to say also that the air staffs of Belgium, Holland, Norway and Denmark were still dominated by the "fighter jockey" mentality, and could not bring themselves to see that an aircraft without a Mach 2 performance at the tropopause could be of any use to anyone. They did not, or did not wish to, understand the operational philosophy behind Jaguar. In the course of promoting this concept in Europe, the principal people who were directly concerned in

Above: BAC and Breguet gained permission from Jaguar Cars to call their new aircraft Jaguar, and the car company climbed on the publicity band wagon at roll-out of the first prototype, posing two of their then latest models beneath the nose *Image in Industry*

Left: Preparations at the French airfield at Istres for one of the early test flights with E01, the first Jaguar prototype. *Dassault-Breguet*

Right: E01, the first Jaguar prototype, on the airfield at Istres at the time it made its first flight on 8 September 1968, with M. Bernard Witt, chief test pilot of Breguet, at the controls. *Dassault-Breguet*

helping me were, Wg Cdr Keys, Mr Nigel Davidson, BAC representative in Paris, Air Chief Marshal Sir Frederick Rosier, military adviser to BAC, Miss Janet Gulland, military aircraft office, Weybridge, and all members of my staff at Weybridge.

'It is something of a paradox that a great deal of our time and energy was spent in trying to drum up an effective level of support for our efforts in Whitehall — in which we sadly failed.'

M Paul Jaillard, commercial director of Avions Marcel Dassault-Breguet, was associated with the Jaguar project from its beginning and wrote the first draft of the agreement between Breguet and BAC in 1965. He said:

'It has to be remembered that when in 1965 the governments of France and Britain designated Breguet and BAC to be airframe partners in the Jaguar project, we in Breguet did not know BAC, although we had worked in partnership previously with Hawker Siddeley.

'With the government agreement signed in May, we had met BAC by the end of that month, and from that point on, everything began to go very smoothly and very quickly. Getting together was not a major problem for us, because on the French side we were dealing with reliable people in reliable British companies.

'It is true that the requirements on the French Air Force and the Royal Air Force were far from being identical, but these differences were soon reconciled. In the process, the size and weight of the Jaguar were increased, and this in turn increased the cost. But this was offset by the fact that between us we were to build 400 aircraft instead of only 200, as specified by our air force.

Above: E02 parked at Le Bourget in June 1969, ready to take part in that year's Paris air show. The Concorde prototype can be seen just beneath the fuselage.
Brian M. Service

'That period in the summer of 1965 was very active, so much so that our engineering department remained at work right through August, the traditional holiday month in France! We moved with such urgency with our new partners that by the end of 1965 the broad lines of the industrial agreements which were later to be concluded by Sepecat were wrapped up. We in Breguet had, of course, derived a great deal of valuable experience of collaborative projects from our work on developing the Atlantique anti-submarine aircraft with other manufacturers in Europe, so we knew very largely what should and should not be done on such a programme.

'The organisation which was established on the industrial side was a very "light" one. With the task split equally between Breguet and BAC on the airframe, and Turbomeca and Rolls-Royce on the engine, and with the French Government controlling the airframe, and the British Government the engine, the management was entirely symmetrical.

'One other advantage of the organisation was that Sepecat is a "ghost" company, with no permanent staff. When the Jaguar project finishes, Sepecat will disappear, and nobody will go unemployed. This system reduces overheads and will prevent work being made for workers thrown out of jobs, under the well-known British principle of Parkinson's Law.

'A further good decision which was taken at the time when the Jaguar project was established was it would not be administered under international law, but

Above: Jaguar E1, the first production aircraft, and destined for service with the French Air Force, after roll-out at the French final assembly works at Toulouse.
Dassault-Breguet

that the airframe should come under French rules, and the engine under British rules. Both had existed for a long time and were well understood. The British ministerial staff soon found to their surprise that the French system was pretty efficient.

'Although it was a two-nation programme, we found that language was not a real problem. Because we at Breguet had trained for exporting, everybody at management level spoke some English. In the design and engineering department shops we found that people were able to reach a mutual understanding by writing down figures on blackboards, and drawing little diagrams. Then there was the problem of our metric system up against your feet and inches. The prototype was virtually hand-built, and the English system was followed for the part made by BAC, and the metric system for the part made by Breguet.

'But this could obviously not continue into the production phase, and so we asked the government departments involved to say which system should be followed. This was the period, in 1968, when Britain had decided to go metric, and we expected the British to say that the Jaguar should be metric also. But surprisingly, the opposite occurred.

'All the measurements we use on Jaguar are to the English system, although they are also given in metric. The French Air Force has come to live with the English system without any major problem, and this simplifies the common logistics arrangements which the FAF has with the RAF on Jaguar.

'The Jaguar project produced many rewarding friendships on both sides of the Channel; names that stand out as cornerstones include, on our side, M Vallieres and General Ziegler, and on the British side, Sir Frederick Page, and Jeffrey Quill. Much has been made over the years about disagreements between the two sides over foreign sales of the Jaguar, and it has been alleged that Dassault tried to block such sales with sales of our own aircraft. But it must be remembered that at the merger of Breguet and Dassault in 1971, the Jaguar was included in the Dassault collection of aircraft, and this created a difficult and controversial situation. The British proposed a world-wide survey of areas where Jaguar sales would be proposed, and where Dassault would not propose the sales of any other aircraft, but this was not acceptable on the French side. Instead, there is an arrangement that British Aerospace is responsible for selling the Jaguar on behalf of the two partners. They know what the French are doing, so that this does not put them into an awkward position when they are dealing with a prospective customer.

'The British have been selling the Jaguar in India, and this began in 1967 as a common Sepecat effort. They took 11 years to come up with a conclusion of the order. It is going well, but at the same time, the Indians have an interest in higher-performance aircraft for high altitude operation, which Jaguar does not satisfy. This situation has been used by some people as a lever against either side in the negotiation of contracts, but in my view, it has not created major difficulties between our two companies at either management or working level. After all, if British Aerospace could sell an all-British aircraft to the Indians, or anywhere else abroad, I have no doubt that they would be only too pleased to do so.'

2 Cross-Channel Accord

Jaguar's inception can be traced back to the year 1962 when, with the Anglo-French Concorde project just starting up, cross-Channel aerospace cooperation was all the rage. Both the Royal Air Force and the French Air Force — the *Armee de l'Air* — started to carry out independent studies for the future of their needs for an advanced trainer, in the French case to take pilots from the simple Fouga Magister to the advanced Mirage 111, and in the British case to replace both the Gnat and the Hunter. Both sides saw the aircraft which would emerge having a secondary role in tactical strike. France planned to have theirs in service by 1970, the British about five years later than that. The British requirement was embodied in AST (Air Staff Target) 362.

As the 1960s progressed, both air forces, once again independently, started to increase the importance of the tactical role and diminish that of the trainer. AST 362 resulted in a number of submissions from British design teams, including Hawker, English Electric, Supermarine, Hunting and Folland. Some of these famous names had already been incorporated into the two big aerospace groups, Hawker Siddeley and British Aircraft Corporation, which were being formed at that time, but their design teams were still at work.

But before any one of these designs could be chosen, the politicians had begun to indicate what an excellent idea it might be if Britain and France got together to develop an aircraft for what was, after all, very similar needs. The idea was attractive in Whitehall and at Westminster because it was felt that a joint project could further Britain's entry chances into the Common Market, while the Concorde co-project was going well at that stage. Meanwhile, the French had started their own competition for a design to meet their requirements. Entries came from Potez, Sud Aviation, Dassault, Breguet and Nord Aviation. Each had been asked to plan a machine costing no more than half a million pounds a copy with a top speed of Mach 1.1. It had to be in service as a trainer by 1970. A tactical version was to follow by 1972. Breguet's design, the Br121, was chosen by the French Air Staff at the end of 1964 as winner of the ECAT (Ecole de

Below: From the looks on the faces of the ground crew, all seems to be going well as this French-assembled Jaguar is readied for a test sortie from Istres. *Dassault-Breguet*

Combat d'Appui Tactique) competition, but by then, serious talks between the British and French on a joint venture had begun.

An operational requirement of a very provisional nature had in fact been circulated to the industries on both sides of the Channel in the spring of 1964, specifying a fairly advanced aircraft with both training and strike capability. At that stage, the French seemed to be more interested in the strike role and the RAF (and the Royal Navy) in the trainer. By October that year, the provisional requirement had been firmed up considerably. Faced with up to 10 different designs from both sides, the joint selection committee which by that time had been formed had a difficult task, especially as considerations of national pride were entering into the choice. Inevitably, a compromise was decided upon. Breguet's Br121 would become the basis for Jaguar, but to smooth any ruffled feathers on the British side, the English Electric team's P45 swing-wing design from the Warton drawing office would form the basis for another joint project, the AFVG — Anglo-French Variable Geometry fighter. This was to be a far more powerful aircraft than the Jaguar, and a memorandum of understanding signed by both governments on 17 May, 1965, covered both the Jaguar and AFVG projects, with British Aircraft Corporation nominated as the British airframe partner, and Breguet and Dassault respectively the French airframe partners. The French were to have design leadership over the Jaguar, the British on AFVG.

The engine for the Jaguar had been firmed up in the previous February when Rolls-Royce and the French company Turbomeca agreed to work jointly to develop a powerplant based on the Rolls RB172. This had already been selected by Breguet for its Br121 before the two sides got together, but Turbomeca had submitted a design of its own, the T-260 Turmolet. Rolls and Turbomeca decided to blend the two designs to a degree in the RB172/T-260, and this then became known as the Adour, after a French river, following Rolls-Royce custom of naming their engines after British rivers. The choice of the Adour for the Jaguar was enshrined in the memorandum of understanding of May 1965, mentioned earlier.

The early agreement between both sides indicated that each would purchase 150 aircraft, with the RAF having only trainers (known as the B, or bi-place version) and the French 75E (for école, or trainer) versions and 75A (for appui, or tactical support) versions. What the French were looking for in the latter version

Below: French-assembled Jaguar E02 arrives at Warton on 9 September 1971, after a 600-mile flight from the Breguet airfield at Cazaux, near Bordeaux, in one hour and 35 minutes. It was flown by Paul Millett, chief test pilot of BAC's military division, and Brian McCann, navigator. E02 joined the test programme at Warton with the British-assembled single seaters S06 and S07, and the first two-seat prototype built to RAF specifications, B08. E02 was the first two-seat trainer for the French Air Force. It carried out engine development test flying from Warton. *BAe*

was a specialised aircraft which could operate in advance of their strike force, softening up targets such as anti-aircraft missile and radar sites, while the RAF wanted a more all-round machine. As a result of British demands, particularly on the need for supersonic performance, the original Br121 design was extensively modified. The wing section was thinned so that higher speeds could be achieved, the weight went up and the engine thrust increased to accommodate the navigation/attack system which the RAF wanted, and the sightlines from the rear cockpit to be used by the instructor were improved through a redesign of the front fuselage. By the end of the 1960s, the French had cancelled the AFVG, claiming shortage of development funds. It was a decision which caused some bitterness in Britain, particularly as it was seen soon after that Dassault was developing a design for a similar aircraft on its own. The loss of the AFVG from the projected inventory of the RAF, together with the TSR2 bomber, and the HS 1154 supersonic vertical take-off fighter projects, both of which were cancelled, left large gaps in the future strike power of the Service, gaps which could only be filled by uprating the offensive role of the Jaguar.

Early in 1967, there was an amendment to the memorandum of understanding which raised the total of Jaguars to be bought by each side from 150 to 200, and out of the British 200, 90 were to be made to a new S (strike) standard. The remaining 110 would all be trainers. The additional 50 which were to go to France were earmarked for the French Navy — the *Aeronavale*. Of these, 10 would be two-seats and the other 40 a new single-seat maritime version coded the M. By 1970, the RAF's requirement had been revised once more; this time its 200 aircraft would consist of only 35 trainers and 165 strike single-seats. At that stage in the Jaguar story, there were five versions being

Above: Jaguar S2 prototype makes a short landing with tail parachute streamed after a test sortie from Warton. The aircraft is carrying a reconnaissance pack and long-range tanks. *BAe*

developed. These were:

Jaguar E, for advanced training with the French Air Force; no in-flight refuelling provision; two Martin Baker Mark IV ejection seats; two DEFA 30mm cannon; five external stores points; twin gyro platform with compass facility; no automatic nav equipment; TACAN and independent gyro gunsight; land arrester hook stressed to 2g.

Jaguar A, single-seat French strike version; provision for in-flight refuelling; Mark IV MB ejection seat; two DEFA cannon; five external stores points; nav/attack system similar to that in Mirage IV, with twin gyro platform and Doppler giving inputs to nav and bombing computers; computer for Martel air-to-surface missile; air data computer; TACAN, VOR/ILS and ECM; 2g arrester.

Jaguar M, single-seat for the French Navy; undercarriage strengthened from 11.8ft/sec of all other versions to 19ft/sec; single main wheels and twin nosewheel (as opposed to twin main wheels and single nosewheel on other versions); arrester hook stressed to 5.5g; Mark IX MB ejection seat for zero-zero operation; provision for in-flight refuelling and also for acting as in-flight refuelling with transfer buddy pack; two DEFA cannon; nav/attack system similar to Jaguar A, but with addition of laser rangefinder; structure strengthened to withstand catapult forces.

Jaguar S, single-seat version for the RAF (designated Jaguar GR Mark 1); in-flight refuelling provision; Mark IX MB ejection seat giving safe ejection at zero speed and zero height; two Aden 30mm

Above: Waiting for take-off clearance to take part in the 1970 Farnborough air display, this French-assembled Jaguar carries long-range tanks and the mock-up of a missile. *Brian M. Service*

cannon; five external stores points; nav/attack system based on inertial platform and central nav digital computer, projected moving-map display, head-up display, laser rangefinding; TACAN; 2g arrester.

Jaguar B, two-seat trainer for the RAF (designated Jaguar T Mark 2); no in-flight refuelling provision; one Aden cannon; Mark IX MB ejection seats; stores points and nav/attack system to same standard as Jaguar S; no laser rangefinder; 2g arrester.

The Jaguar project was claimed to be the first in the world between two countries to produce a combat aircraft. The 1965 memorandum of understanding called for the formation of a joint Anglo-French industrial company to administer the design and manufacture. This was duly registered in France in May 1966, as SEPECAT, which stands for Societe Europeene de Production de l'Avion Ecole de Combat et d'Appui Tactique. SEPECAT operations were to be supervised by an Anglo-French management committee of officials. This had four members representing, for Britain, the Ministry of Technology and the Ministry of Defence and, for France, the Delegation Ministerelle pour l' Armement, and the Etat-Major de l'Armee de l'Air et Aeronavale. Three sub-committees reported to the main committee on problems in the areas of airframe, engine and administration. Sales promotion was dealt with separately by a group formed from representatives from the DMA, the Ministry of Technology, and the industrial companies involved.

Jaguar airframe contracts were issued by the DTCA (Direction Technique de Construction Aeronautique) a French government organisation acting as executive authority for both the British and French governments, while a complementary organisation was established on the Adour engine, with the Ministry of Technology as executive authority. A British-registered company, Rolls-Royce Turbomeca Ltd, was established to administer the industrial manufacture of the engine. The partner governments claimed at the time that there were several benefits flowing from an industrial organisation like that which was established for Jaguar. Apart from receiving contracts, SEPECAT provided a single unified industrial body with whom overseas customers negotiated (the post of president was filled in alternate years by M B. C. Vallieres, chairman and managing director of Breguet Aviation, and Mr F. W. Page (now Sir Frederick Page) at that time chairman and managing director of BAC Preston division). For the purpose of the execution of the contracts entered into by SEPECAT and DTCA, SEPECAT had at its disposal the design, manufacturing, financial and administrative facilities of both Breguet and BAC. The board of SEPECAT had appointed representatives from the technical, production, financial and sales departments of each company, and these together constituted the SEPECAT management committee. A single chain of command in SEPECAT was maintained in each of these activities by designating Breguet as leaders in matters of design and production, with BAC leading in matters of finance and sales.

The original agreement on Jaguar between the two countries stipulated that the expenditure and the content of new technology in the project should be divided equally, and this direction was scrupulously followed. In the manufacture of the airframe, the nose and centre fuselage was made by Breguet, plus the

Above: S06, first Jaguar to be produced to RAF specifications, on flight trials prior to delivery to the Service. *BAe*

undercarriage, and the wings and tail unit, rear fuselage and engine intakes by BAC. These items were then exchanged between two identical production lines, in France and Britain. French aircraft were assembled at Colomiers, on Toulouse-Blagnac airport, south-west France. This division of effort applied to all prototypes and production aircraft, whether they were destined for France, Britain, or export customers. Work on the engine was split in a similar manner. Rolls-Royce producing the combustion chamber, turbine, mixer and other components, and Turbomeca, producing the low and high-pressure compressors, the intermediate case, the gearbox, afterburner and jet nozzle assembly. The engines were assembled on two lines, one at Derby, England, the other at Tarnos, France.

A 'partner companies' brief issued in 1968 explained why a twin-engine configuration had been chosen, despite the extra cost, both initial and operating, over one. 'In a twin-engine aircraft', it said, 'the probability of getting home after an engine failure, due to enemy fire or other causes, is much higher than in a single-engined machine. World statistics covering several millions of flight hours, show that for aircraft of similar characteristics and wing loading, the accident rate is two and one half times higher with single-engine than with twin-engine aircraft. The consequent savings in cost are considerable; for the same operational strength, the number of single-engine aircraft to be ordered has to be 30% higher than the number of twin-engine ones.'

Jaguar had been designed to achieve: short take-off from roughly-prepared fields which had a grass or compacted soil surface, a basic tactical mission of long range on internal fuel alone, good overload capability, docile handling characteristics, efficient high-lift devices, good accessibility to reduce maintenance and servicing costs, development potential, including a naval aircraft, and flexibility in the choice of a weapon system without disturbing the basic aircraft systems, which remained common to all versions. Development potential, stated the partner manufacturers, included increased speed, higher payloads and improved airfield performance to be made possible by increased engine thrust and the use of variable geometry intakes.

In the maintenance and ground-handling sectors, the design aims were, simple engine change — achieveable in 30 minutes, including run-up time — access to engine without step ladder, plug-in type of equipment to be easily replaced, 15-minute turnround, including rearming. Maximum speeds were predicted as, Mach 1.1 at low altitude and Mach 1.7 at high altitude, and radii of action as follows: (figures achieved by Jaguar International in brackets) lo-lo-lo mission (with internal fuel) 650km (535), (with external fuel) 850km (915); hi-lo-hi (with internal fuel) 1,250km (1,850), (with external fuel) 1,650km (1,410); ferry (with external fuel) 4,500km.

In a training sortie of one and a half hours at low altitude, 20 minutes would be available at Mach 0.9 and one hour 10 minutes at Mach 0.7. At high altitude the sortie duration at high altitude would be three hours, or in a sortie of two hours and 10 minutes duration, ten minutes would be available at supersonic speed. Take-off and landing performances, carrying a typical tactical load of four 1,000lb bombs were given as: distance to clear 50ft (15m) obstacle 720m (880), ground roll 450m (565); landing, distance to clear 50ft obstacle 860m, ground roll 470m. Maximum nominal dry thrust of the Adour engine was to be in excess of 2,000kg (4,400lb), with maximum reheat thrust in

ision, watched the first flight closely from an accompanying chase aircraft. Witt, at that time aged 42, had flown around 8,000 hours in all types of aircraft and had had a distinguished aviation career as a test pilot in several French government establishments. Among the new aircraft he had had the responsibility of testing were the supersonic Taon, the Breguet 940 and 941 short take-off and landing prototypes, and the Atlantique maritime reconnaissance aircraft.

On 11 February 1969, the second Jaguar prototype made its maiden flight, also from Istres, and went supersonic. Once again the pilot was Witt. On this occasion he was airborne for 65 minutes, after which he commented, 'I am very pleased with the aeroplane. First impression of E02 confirms the excellent flying qualities of the first prototype'. Witt reached 30,000ft on this sortie. Like E01, the E02 prototype was a two-seater, and by the time of its maiden flight E01 had been flown numerous times by Witt, Dell and pilots from the Centre d'Essais En Vol, at Istres, the French air force, and the Aeroplane and Armament Experimental Establishment at Boscombe Down.

The first single-seat Jaguar prototype flew for the first time on 29 March 1969, with the code A03. Once again Bernard Witt was at the controls and the airfield was once again Istres. The Jaguar was airborne for 70 minutes. 'Excellent results have been obtained so far from the flight test programme', BAC and Breguet said in a joint statement — 'particularly in the handling qualities of the aeroplane and its performance'. Assembly of the fifth prototype (M05) to French navy specifications had by that time begun. Codes for the eight prototypes were by this time firmed up as follows — French versions: E01 and E02 two-seat trainers, A03 and A04 single-seat tactical attack aircraft, M05 single-seat carrier-based tactical attack aircraft; British versions: S06 and S07 single-seat tactical attack aircraft, B08 two-seat trainer. The first four aircraft were used as follows: E01 for general systems testing, control and handling qualities and flutter trials, E02 for engine optimisation and flight performance tests, A03 for testing and evaluation of the navigation and attack systems for the French versions, and A04 for weapon and stores carriage and weapon-firing

3 Prototypes, Prototypes

The agreement covering the production of the Jaguar was signed in London on 9 January 1968, by Denis Healey, the then British Secretary of State for Defence, John Stonehouse, the then British Minister of State for Technology, and Pierre Messmer, the then French Ministre des Armees. The agreement provided for an initial production programme of 400 aircraft, half for each government, with the production work to be shared between British and French aircraft companies. By that time the first prototype was practically complete and was expected to fly that spring. Both sides cited the signing as, 'an indication of the successful development of the aircraft, and of the faith which the UK and French governments have in its future.'

It was, in fact, August that year before the first of seven Jaguar prototypes completed preliminary taxi trials at the French flight test centre at Istres, near Marseilles. Modifications of a fairly minor nature were found to be necessary, but the time needed to carry these out meant that the new aircraft missed appearing at the 1968 Farnborough air show. First flight eventually took place on 8 September from Istres with the chief test pilot for Breguet, Bernard Witt, at the controls. Witt took off at 9.20am (wind six knots, outside air temperature 21°C) and took the aircraft up to 17,000ft. On landing after a flight of 25 minutes (block-to-block time was 40 minutes) Witt said, 'Jaguar flies very well. I had no problems'. The maiden flight was watched, by among others, the president of Breguet, M Vallieres, and the managing director of British Aircraft Corporation's Preston division F. W. Page. Both were said to have been, 'well pleased.' Jimmy Dell, chief test pilot of the BAC Preston div-

Right: At the Farnborough air show in the autumn of 1980, BAe revealed a maritime version of the Jaguar (pictured on the ground here, as a Jaguar International flies past). It was to have the Thomson CSF Agave multi-purpose radar and carry anti-shipping missiles and long-range tanks. In addition Maritime-Jaguar would have the capability of being armed with Matra Magic missiles on overwing stations. At the time of writing, there were no buyers. *BAe*

excess of 3,000kg (6,600lb). Estimated time between overhaul was put at 1,000 hours.

The official description of Jaguar was, an all-metal, shoulder wing aircraft with high-lift devices. Control was by wing spoilers, all-moving tailplane and rudder. Sizes and weights: wingspan 8.488m (8.69), length (tactical version) 15.520m, (trainer) 16.420m, height 4.640m (4.89), wing area 24sq m (24.18), aspect ratio 3.00, (3.12), wing sweepback 40 degrees, normal take-off weight 10,000kg (11,000), maximum take-off weight 13,500kg (15.500), weapon load 4,500kg (4,700), wheel base 5.670m (5.73), track 2.400m, main wheels tyre size 615, tyre pressure 3.8 bar (5.0), nose wheel tyre size 550, tyre pressure 2.7 bar (3.5).

To enable the aircraft to operate from rough fields, the undercarriage was designed to accept a vertical velocity of 3.6m/sec. Ejection seats were to be Martin Baker Mark IV or Mark IX. The stores choice included air-to-surface guided missiles AS 30 or AS 37 (Martel), air-to-air guided missiles of the Sidewinder type, two 30mm guns, all sizes of high-explosive bombs, all types of unguided rockets, an external reconnaissance pack, flares, and external fuel tanks. Flight controls were mechanically linked to power control jack rams working in tandem within a double body. These actuated the rudder, the all-moving tailplane, and the spoilers. Yaw and roll artificial feel were obtained by means of springs, the load varying as a function of control movement. Artificial feel in pitch took into account both flight conditions and control movement. The trim system about the three axes was such that trim runaway was not dangerous. Provisions had been made for yaw and pitch damping if wanted.

Armour was used at the front of the cockpit and on the underside of the tactical version. The windshield would be proof against rifle calibre fire. Self-sealing liners were used for the fuel tanks, and the fuel lines themselves were armoured.

Above: S06, first Jaguar for the RAF, comes in for a landing at BAC Warton after flight trials. *BAE*

Below: In the middle of 1975, BAC began flying S3 with the uprated Mark 804 Adour, and Tim Ferguson, BAC's military aircraft deputy chief test pilot was quoted after the first two sorties as saying that Jaguar now had the performance of an interceptor. The uprated Adour gave Jaguar improved time-to-height performance and a better sustained g capability. For take-off, there was a 27% enhancement of thrust. *BAe*

trials. A04 flew for the first time on 27 May 1969, with Jimmy Dell at the controls. The flight was again from Istres, and the time airborne was 45 minutes.

The new type began to make its first public appearances at around this time — at the Paris salon at Le Bourget in front of the French public, and at the Central Flying School of the Royal Air Force at Little Rissington in Britain. In the latter case the aircraft was one of the single-seat prototypes, and was supported by a French ground crew. It was flown by Dell as part of the 57th anniversary celebrations of the CFS in the presence of the Queen, the Queen Mother, and the Duke of Edinburgh.

The first British-assembled prototype — S06 — was rolled out at BAC's factory at Warton, Lancashire, on 18 August 1969 and flew for the first time nearly two months later, on 12 October. It went supersonic on this maiden outing. Jimmy Dell was the pilot, the flight lasting for 50 minutes. The following month, on 14 November, M05, the French maritime prototype made its maiden flight from the airfield at Melun-Villaroche. The Breguet Aviation test pilot Jaques Jesberger was at the controls, and the flight lasted for 30 minutes.

With six prototypes now on the flight line in France and Britain, the test programme began to accelerate. By February 1970, they had accumulated 326 hours in 332 flights, and BAC and Breguet said that the results obtained were 'extremely satisfactory' and that the aircraft had been shown to have 'excellent flying

Far left, top: Flying just on top of the cloud layer, two Jaguars on test from Warton wheel away from the camera 'plane. Nearest the camera is S06; behind is S07. *BAe*

This page and bottom left: During rough field trials at Boscombe down, B08, loaded with four 1,000lb bombs and two equipment pods, lands and takes off from a grass strip, and taxies sedately through an uncut meadow. *BAe*

Above left: Maritime prototype M05, carrying a heavy load of hardware, is coaxed on to the steam catapult on board the French aircraft carrier *Clemenceau.* *BAe*

Left: And away she goes. Steam billows up from the catapult as M05, reheats blazing, thunders off the deck of the *Clemenceau.* *Dassault-Breguet*

Below: B08 prototype about to unstick on a test sortie out of Warton carries, in addition to long-range tanks, 1,000lb retarded bombs on the outboard pylons and on the centreline stations. *BAe*

tions differed from the rest because most of the airframe was made up of production parts, enabling it to be flight-tested towards production standard. The flight thus marked an important landmark in the Anglo-French programme, BAC said. The first production Jaguar took off for the first time from Toulouse/Blagnac airport on 2 November. Once again Bernard Witt was at the controls, and the sortie on this occasion lasted 35 minutes. Up to that moment the eight prototypes had flown a total of 2,300 hours in 1,350 flights. The two partner airframe companies took the opportunity to confirm their view that first deliveries to the French air force would begin in early 1972 and to the RAF early the following year.

It was almost a year later, on 12 October 1972, that the first production Jaguar for the RAF made its maiden flight. It took off from Warton with Tim Ferguson, deputy chief test pilot of the BAC military aircraft division in charge and was airborne for an hour and 11 minutes, part of that time supersonic. Just over a month later, on 16 November, the second production aircraft for the RAF took off for a 75-minute maiden flight, including a supersonic burst, with Paul Millett 'up'. This aircraft, coded S2, was the first to be fitted with the laser ranger and marked target seeker fitted in the nose as part of an avionics package which, BAC claimed, would give Jaguar a target location and weapon delivery accuracy better than any other existing European combat aircraft. Information from the airborne laser, together with other data such as height and speed, was fed into the on-board computer, which continually recomputed the target and kept the target marker on it. Weapons were released automatically after pre-selection by the pilot. When an attack had been completed, the whole system was designed to revert to the task of navigation for the escape from the target area ready for another attack, or return to base.

Above: Banking away from the camera over a snow-covered landscape, the S07 prototype shows off its portside airbrake and its ventral fins. It is hauling long-range tanks and two 1,000lb practice bombs. *BAe*

Below: In this impressive nose-on shot, Jaguar prototype S07 is loaded with four 1,000lb retarded bombs, four Matra 155 rocket launchers, and a 264gal fuel tank under the fuselage. *BAe*

S2 was used early in 1973 for stores clearance flying. It lifted a variety of hardware during these trials, including in one sortie four 1,000lb bombs and two 264gal fuel tanks. By that time the eight prototypes and early production aircraft had between them notched up a total of over 2,000 flights. E02 had been transferred, on flight No 191 in the programme on 9 September 1971, from Cazaux, France, to Warton, to facilitate engine development flight trials. The aircraft remained in Britain until 1980.

4 Green Light from France

By February 1973 the Jaguar was approaching the point where it would go into squadron service with the French, and on the 22nd of that month the Chief of Staff of the French Air Force, General Claude Grigaut, went to the Centre of Military Aircraft Evaluation (CEAM) at Mont-de-Marsan to fly it. Afterwards, he gave it the green light, commenting for public consumption:

'It is a straightforward aircraft of great reliability, and it handles extremely well. Operationally speaking, it complies exactly with the French operational requirements, which called for medium and low-altitude performance.

'It meets the short take-off and landing requirement, although this has tended to complicate the design somewhat. At the same time, it is capable of high speeds, good manoeuvrability at low altitudes, and extensive range, and supersonic capability.'

The general was asked if teething problems had been rectified. 'Like all prototypes, there have been problems, but these have been cleared up, and the aircraft is OK,' he replied. Jaguar would replace obsolescent aircraft such as the Vautour, the SMB2, and gradually some early Mirages. It would be, 'next year's defence aircraft'. Compared with the Mirage F1 it had additional characteristics in respect of low-speed handling and landing approach, because of its aerodynamic features. Fuel capacity was greater, and it could fly longer in supersonic flight. It had, 'new-generation equipment', including automatic defect testing.

The months after the general's flight came the announcement that the first Jaguar squadron was to form in May, at Saint Dizier, in eastern France. Deliveries to the RAF were scheduled to begin at about the same time, but the first aircraft was to be used at RAF Lossiemouth by the recently-formed Service school for ground training. Deliveries of flying aircraft were to begin to the RAF in August, and the first batch would include at least one two-seat trainer.

Below: Two halves of a Jaguar are about to be slotted together at Warton *BAe*

XX753
PS650
NO STEP
NO STEP
NO STEP

XX754
PS651

Above left: A further view of the Warton assembly line, with Jaguars, already mated from sections made in Britain and France, in the final stages. *BAe*

Left: Final assembly of Jaguars at BAC's military aircraft division factory at Warton, Lancashire. *BAe*

Above: French Jaguar production in full swing. The photograph shows forward fuselages coming down the line. *BAe*

By the time of this announcement, in May 1973, Jaguars had completed some 3,000 test flights and over 3,000 flight hours. Five hundred of these sorties had been made by Jaguars in French Air Force service from the centre at Mont de Marsan. Twenty production Jaguars had flown on both sides of the Channel, and in France 12 had been accepted, with a further four awaiting acceptance.

First delivery to the RAF took place at Lossiemouth on 30 May 1973, S4 arriving before official release to give the RAF ground-handling experience. A week before that, the Service's seal of approval was placed on its new aircraft when the Vice Chief of the Air Staff, Air Marshal Sir Denis Smallwood, flew in B1* the first production two-seater, from the BAC airfield at Warton. In charge was Paul Millett, BAC's chief test pilot at Warton. During the sortie, which lasted one hour, the Jaguar's advanced navigation and weapon-aiming systems were demonstrated to the air marshal. The aircraft also made a supersonic run, carried out low-speed manoeuvres, and touched down twice on the Warton runway before coming in to land. Sir Denis said afterwards: 'It really is a superb aeroplane. I was really delighted with it. It is a remarkably straight forward aeroplane to fly. It handled delightfully at supersonic speed. The navigation and weapon-aiming systems were exceptional. The RAF has a tradition of really good aircraft, such as the Spitfire and the Canberra, and the Jaguar is going to be well in keeping with this tradition. We can't wait to get it into the RAF.'

The French Jaguars may have beaten those of the RAF into service, but at the Paris air show which took place at the end of May there was no chagrin visible, senior officers from both the French AF and the RAF sitting down together and talking about their aspirations with the new type. Colonel Brisset, head of the French AF operational requirements staff (aircraft), commented expansively. 'It is a technical success for Franco-British cooperation, and we must congratulate those who designed it, those who kept it alive, and those who made it fit to take its place with its peers.' Jaguar's qualities enabled it to undertake any type of tasks with efficiency, such as direct-fire support, air-superiority at medium-low altitudes with the Matra Magic missile in FAF service, collection of information on the battlefield, destruction of surface raiders, penetration at low altitude, and tactical nuclear tasks like armed intervention behind the lines. 'Jaguar is a

* B1 was subsequently lost on a test flight from ARAEE Boscombe Down.

S.W.L. 1 TON AT 310 CENTRES
S.W.L. 1 TON AT 310 CENTRES
A4
E7

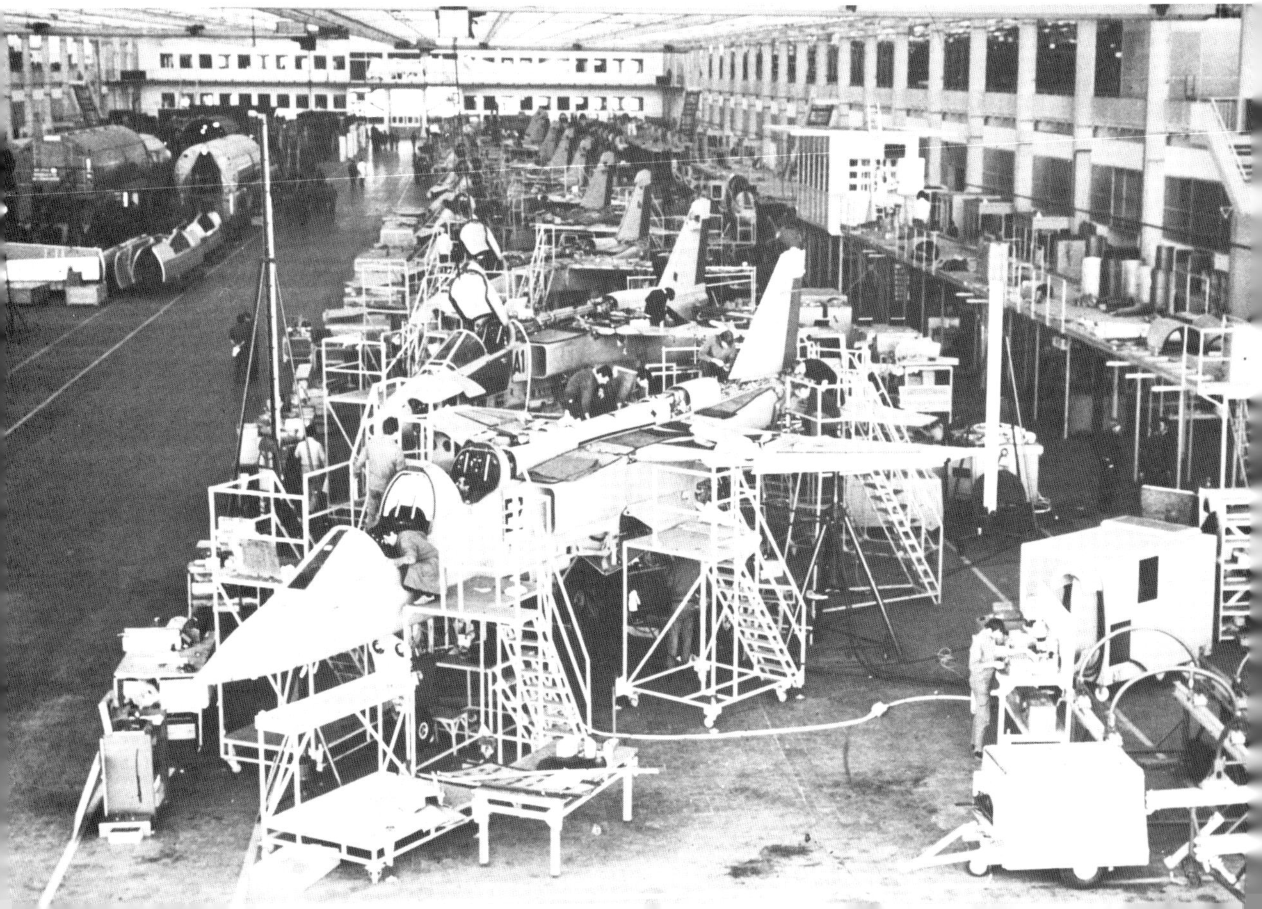

Left: French production in full swing. Rear fuselages and fins of the fourth strike aircraft and seventh trainer aircraft for the FAF; and virtually-complete two-seats and single-seats. *Dassault-Breguet*

Right: The nose and centre fuselage of Jaguar S1, the first single-seat for the RAF, arrives at Warton from France in May 1972. Deliveries to the French Air Force had begun earlier that month. *BAe*

solidly-built aircraft, easy to maintain and handle. It goes a long way quickly, and constitutes an excellent firing platform. It carries an impressive array of weapons systems, well adapted to medium-low altitudes.'

Gp Capt David Toon, Deputy Director Operational Requirements, spoke for the RAF. He said:

'We are particularly pleased with the performance shown by Jaguar. It will replace the Phantom FGR2 in the strike/attack and tactical reconnaissance roles, providing a strong contribution to NATO, and will be based in the UK and Germany. Jaguar can carry significant loads of weapons over considerable distances at high speed. It has a good fire power, and will be equipped not only with conventional weapons, but some of them could have a nuclear capability to replace the strike side of Phantom. The excellent nav/attack system in Jaguar, incorporating digital computer and laser ranging, gives the aircraft target and weapon delivery accuracy which we believe second to none.

'Pilot conversion training will begin in October 1973, in time for the formation of the first of the RAF squadrons in the spring of 1974. The first production Jaguars, two single-seat and one two-seat versions, are currently involved in acceptance trials at Boscombe Down prior to issue of contracts of aircraft's release to the RAF at the end of July. Results to date are most encouraging, and the aircraft is proving particularly easy to maintain, because of the emphasis given in the design to ease of access to engines, equipment bays, and control circuits. The Jaguar is the first collaborative combat aircraft ever to enter service and we, like our French partners, are pleased to go Jaguar.'

The following month — June 1973 — ceremonies were held at the French AF base at Saint Dizier to mark the aircraft's official entry into service. It was a glittering occasion, with guests representing the partner airframe, engine and equipment manufacturers, the two governments, and the Services from either side. An impressive force of ten of the new aircraft were lined up for inspection. Commandant Max Simon, in charge of the first French squadron, showed off the Jaguar's flying capabilities. The guest of honour on that day was the then French Minister of Armed Forces, M. Robert Galley, who described Jaguar as being 'Among the foremost penetration aircraft in the French Air Force'. The minister also went out of his way to stress the importance of economies which, he said, had been gained from international collaboration, and emphasised that there were years of development ahead for the design. General Grigaut said in his speech, 'At low altitude, the Jaguar carries an unprecedented weapon load over distances never

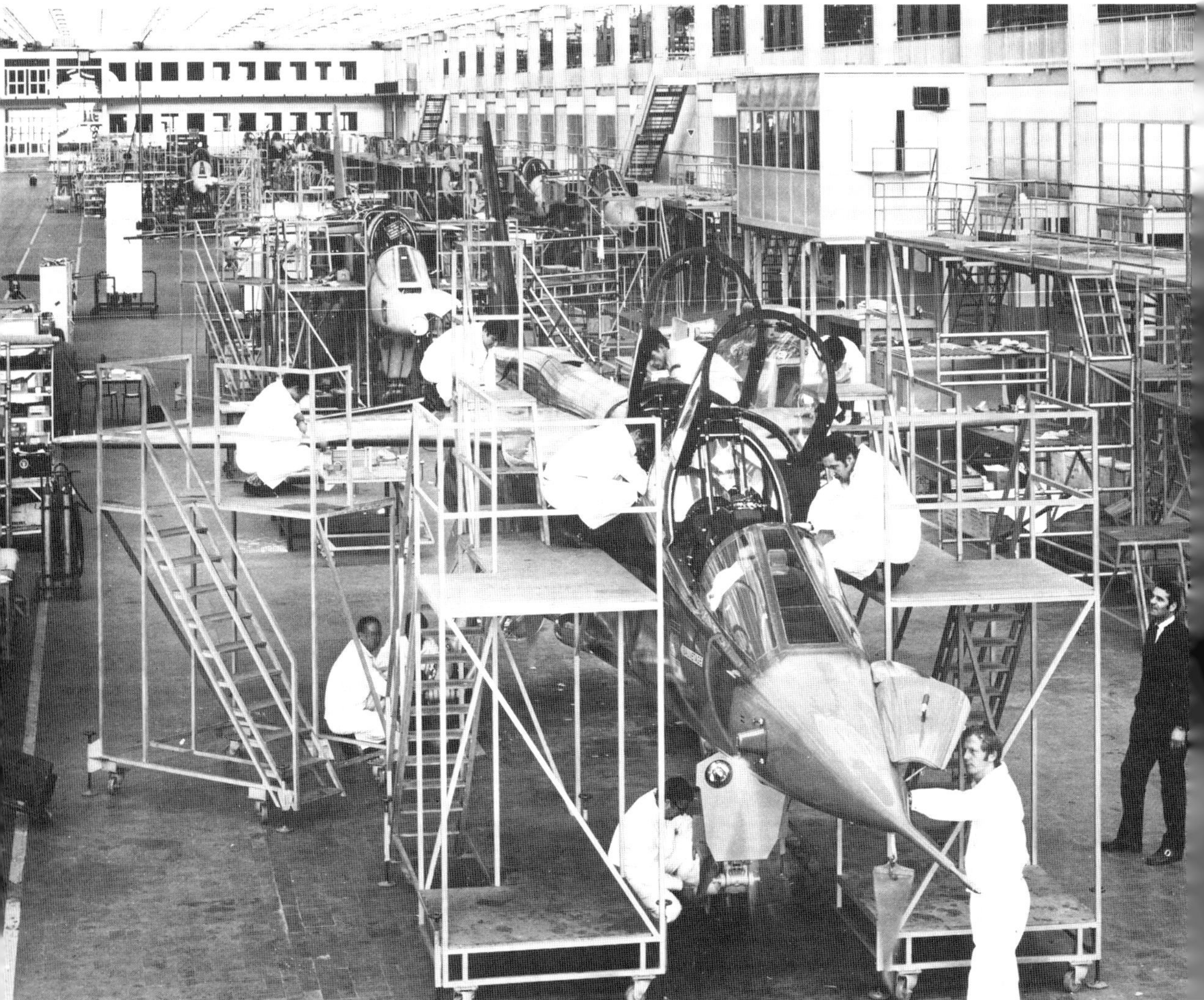

yet reached by a French tactical aircraft'. At the same time, the heavy security veil which had shrouded the project began to lift, and it was indicated that the weapons payload from short runways was in the region of 10,000lb, and that radius of action came out at around 800 miles.

Air Chief Marshal Sir Lewis Hodges, deputy Commander-in-Chief, Allied Forces, Central Europe, described the Jaguar's stability at high speed as, 'outstanding', and said that the aircraft was, 'A joy to fly', when he took a 45-minute ride in B1 with Paul Millett from Warton in August 1973. 'I was most impressed with its performance and its handling,' he added. Further bouquets came in May 1974, when Roy Mason, then British Secretary of State for Defence, visited RAF Lossiemouth, where Jaguar was being introduced into the Service, with No 54 Squadron. It was, he said, beating all records on training and testing, 'faster than has ever been done with a similar aircraft', and had already built up an incredibly good record and a great reputation.

Mason went on to make the first public references to the hopes which the joint manufacturers were by that time harbouring that they might sell Jaguar abroad. It was, he suggested, a first-class success story which was going to be an export winner. 'It is a collaborative effort which augurs well for the future. I am satisfied we will sell a great many of them.' Sir Denis Smallwood, by June that year promoted to Air Chief Marshal, and Air Officer Commanding-in-Chief, Strike Command, also gave a glowing progress report: 'We have already done a lot of flying with the Jaguar in the comparatively short time in which we had it in service — well over 1,500 hours from here (Lossiemouth) alone — and everybody, including myself, is delighted with its performance.

'That is not an exaggeration by any means. Its performance has come well up to the expectations of the original specification, not only in its performance in the air, but also particularly on the ground, where the emphasis given to this aeroplane by the designers on the ease of servicing is already showing great dividends in terms of cost-effectiveness in manpower and ease of maintenance. The performance in the air is very highly satisfactory, particularly in terms of the great weapon load which this aircraft can carry, in its conventional capability in particular, in its range and radius in action, and not least, perhaps, on its airfield performance. There is no doubt that the collaborative project has been extremely successful. It is a great achievement.'

Wg Cdr John Walker, officer commanding the Jaguar operational conversion unit at Lossiemouth, described the aircraft as: 'A very high performance little ship. It certainly gets out and gets up very fast indeed — to the point that it surprises Lightning pilots. For the first time we have got an aircraft where you can virtually guarantee, on interdiction-type targets, making the very fast, low-level, straight-pass attack. This must surely be one of the big aids in keeping yourself in one piece. The aim of weapons delivery is to put the bomb on the target, and that's what Jaguar does better than anything else we have. Jaguar is probably the finest pilot's aircraft that many of us have flown.' And on

Top left: Nose sections of Jaguars come down the line at the French production centre in early 1972. *BAe*

Left: Final Jaguar assembly at Breguet's factory at Toulouse, south-west France. *Breguet*

Right: This 1968 shot shows a prototype Adour on test with afterburner operating. *The Times*

reliability . . . 'I don't think we have had an aircraft into service and that has had a record such as the Jaguar. The reliability is so good, in fact, that we are having to put people through special emergency training programmes now, because we are not getting any emergency training in the normal run-of-the-mill training sorties. We are not getting emergencies.'

Wg Cdr Walker also praised the cockpit layout, commenting, 'The designers got the priorities right, right from the start. Everything that matters is in front of you. The pilots like the cockpit. It is a very, very good fighter cockpit'. The electrical system should be a model for future aircraft design, while the accuracy of the navigation system was, 'Very much up to specification in service.' Plans for deployment of the 200 Jaguars ordered for the RAF were also announced on the same occasion. The first squadron, 54, moved from Lossiemouth to its permanent base at Coltishall in late 1974 to form one of nine Jaguar squadrons in the Service. Five of these were assigned exclusively to NATO under the Supreme Allied Commander Europe, two were to be based at Coltishall, and the remaining two were to equip the permanent ops conversion unit at Lossiemouth. When all in service, the Jaguar force accounted for the biggest single element in the front-line strength of the RAF.

Below: Adours for Jaguar on the assembly line at Rolls-Royce. By the middle of 1981, Rolls and their partners Turbomeca had produced a total of 1,500 engines for the Jaguar and Hawk. Total Adour requirements for these programmes, and for manufacture under licence in Japan was 2,500 engines. Adours had, by mid-1981, completed over one million hours in service. *Rolls-Royce*

to a very high standard and was used largely to check engineering design, layout and compatibility. Pylons were installed to test the mounting of stores. Integral wing skins for the prototypes and production aircraft were machined by BAC at its Strand Road, Preston, works from billets of aluminium alloy each measuring 17.9ft by 2.28ft by 1.69in. Each weighed initially 1,705lb before being shaped by numerically-controlled machines into final form when they weighed 227lb for the upper skin and 219lb for the lower structure. Components and assemblies built by the French at Biarritz — front fuselage — and at Toulouse — centre fuselage — were shipped to Britain by sea. Shipping charges for each aircraft were reckoned to be around £2,650, underlining the increased cost of splitting manufacture between two countries. The overall cost of this dispersal was put as high as 20%. Some indication of the 'learning curve' involved can be gained from the fact that the first French prototype took almost a year to build, while the later prototypes came off the final assembly lines in six months. Despite this (although the exact figures were never revealed by either of the partner governments) the unit cost of each Jaguar was reliably estimated at around £1million, a small enough sum even in 1970 aerospace terms. Development costs were put at £50million, split between Britain and France equally, with the airframe accounting for £35million of this and the engine the rest. The production airframe contract for 400 aircraft was worth some £230million, the engine contract some £100million. This assumed an engine unit price of £100,000, with 200 built as spares. Each ship set of radio and nav/attack system was worth some £75,000, and this brought the total cost of the programme to £410million, or a unit cost of a little over the £1million.

Apart from the titanium processes mentioned earlier, the materials and processes used in the manufacture of Jaguar were almost entirely conventional — 85% of the airframe by weight was aluminium alloy in the form of clad sheets, drawn sections and forgings. In addition to the wing, the fin and tailplane torque box skins were machined in solid aluminium alloy — a method designed to give good fatigue properties — and aluminium honeycomb sandwich was used extensively in the front and centre fuselage. Stainless steel was used for highly-stressed components, such as tailplane spigot housing, the fin attachment and pylon mountings. Titanium alloy was used for high-temperature skinning of the engine bay area. The remit given to the design team was to ensure high survivability in case of equipment failure or damage by enemy action, and to this end the aircraft's hydraulic and electrical systems were duplicated. The fuel system had self-sealing collector boxes and protected fuel feed pipes, while the fuel transfer was independent for each tank to give minimum fuel loss in the event of damage to transfer piping or tankage. The windscreen was designed to be proof against small arms fire, or birdstrikes at 600kts.

In the case of the Adour, the designers were told to keep it simple and rugged in order to achieve the target of 1,000 hours between overhauls. The basic layout was twin shaft, with the main components a two-stage low pressure compressor driven by single stage low pressure turbine, and a five stage high pressure compressor driven by a single stage high pressure turbine. The combustion system consisted of a single fully-annular chamber. No inlet guide vanes were fitted so that the engine would be less prone to ingestion problems. By-pass ratio was 1 and the pressure ratio 9.6. The maximum dry thrust of 4,6000lb could be boosted with reheat to 9,600lb, although the degree of reheat used was constantly variable by the pilot. Each engine was suspended on three mountings incorporating spherical bearings. Engine bay doors were attached to the fuselage by means of special pins and could be completely removed. The hinges were lockable in two positions to enable the doors to be held at either 60 degrees or 80 degrees. Engine disconnections could be easily made with the engine doors open, and removal and installation of the engines carried out with the doors open to the 80 degrees position. The original design called for asymmetric recoveries and landings to be made using dry thrust on one engine only, but early development flying experience showed that the margins of safety involved in such operations at high all-up weight were slight. To allow more flexibility, a part throttle reheat system was developed capable of operating within the dry thrust range so that continuous power increase could be maintained without extinguishing or relighting re-heat up to maximum power — so enabling single-engine recoveries to be made at higher weights.

Indication of an engine problem caused the crash of prototype E01 at Istres on 26 March 1970. An engine-bay fire warning light came on during a test flight and the pilot shut down that powerplant, losing the services of one of the two main hydraulic systems. The fire-suppression system was selected. By that time, the aircraft was well over the runway and to get rid of unwanted thrust, the second engine was shut down. But emergency hydraulic power was not selected so that the flying controls froze. The pilot ejected successfully, but the aircraft was written off and was not replaced in the development programme. Another early difficulty experienced with Jaguar during the test flying was with low-speed lateral control. These were overcome by using tail surfaces as elevons — differentially to supplement the lateral spoiler controls which had been built into the design as an option from the start, initially as a spin-recovery aid.

1 Nose detail of two-seat trainer version
2 Pitot probe
3 'Wedge'-profile nose glazing
4 Ferranti laser telemetry unit
5 Air data computer
6 Waveform generator
7 Two total-pressure probes
8 Radio altimeter
9 HF/VHF power amplifier
10 Equipment bay cooling ducts
11 Intake
12 Nav/attack electronics compartments
13 External emergency canopy release
14 Ajax feel unit (pitch control)
15 Nosewheel well
16 Instrument panel
17 Projected map display (head-down)
18 Windscreen
19 Head-up display panel
20 Plexiglass canopy
21 Martin Baker Mk 9 ejector seat
22 Honeycomb cockpit side panels
23 Instrument console
24 Access panels
25 Cannon barrel
26 Battery and electrics bay
27 Intake
28 Spring-loaded supplementary-air doors
29 30mm Aden cannon
30 Main undercarriage side door
31 Undercarriage retraction jack
32 Integrally-stiffened frame
33 Ammunition trough
34 Intake bolt-up joints
35 Intake duct frames
36 Intake/fuselage attachment plate
37 Cold-air unit
38 Ram-air intake
39 Twin VHF homer aerials
40 Inner dorsal spine (hydraulic and cable runs)
41 Slat motor and gearbox
42 264 Imp gallon (1,200-1) auxiliary fuel tank
43 Starboard inner pylon
44 1,000lb (472kg) bomb
45 Starboard outer stores pylon
46 Leading-edge steel slat-rail
47 Starboard navigation light
48 Honeycomb-filled spoiler
49 Wing fence
50 Pylon mount
51 Fuel lines
52 Wing construction
53 Starboard wing integral fuel tank
54 Dorsal anti-collision beacon
55 Control rods
56 Wing centre-joint
57 Forward wing-fixing joint
58 Ram-air intake
60 Honeycomb-filled flap
61 Primary heat-exchanger
62 Upper fuselage access panels
63 Engine forward mounting point
64 Accumulator No 2 system
65 Hydraulic system pressure reservoir No 2
66 Air extractor duct
67 Upper fuselage access panels
68 Inward/outward vent valve
69 Starboard/tailplane
70 Tailfin construction
71 Magnetic detector
72 Tailfin leading-edge
73 Sensor fairing
74 VHF/UHF antenna in fin tip
76 Rear navigation light
77 HF antenna
78 Honeycomb-filled rudder section
79 Fuel dump vent
80 Landing parachute housing
81 Rudder power control unit
82 Control run linkage
83 Tailplane control units
84 Tailplane pivot point
85 Tailplane construction
86 Tailplane longitudinal stability discontinuity

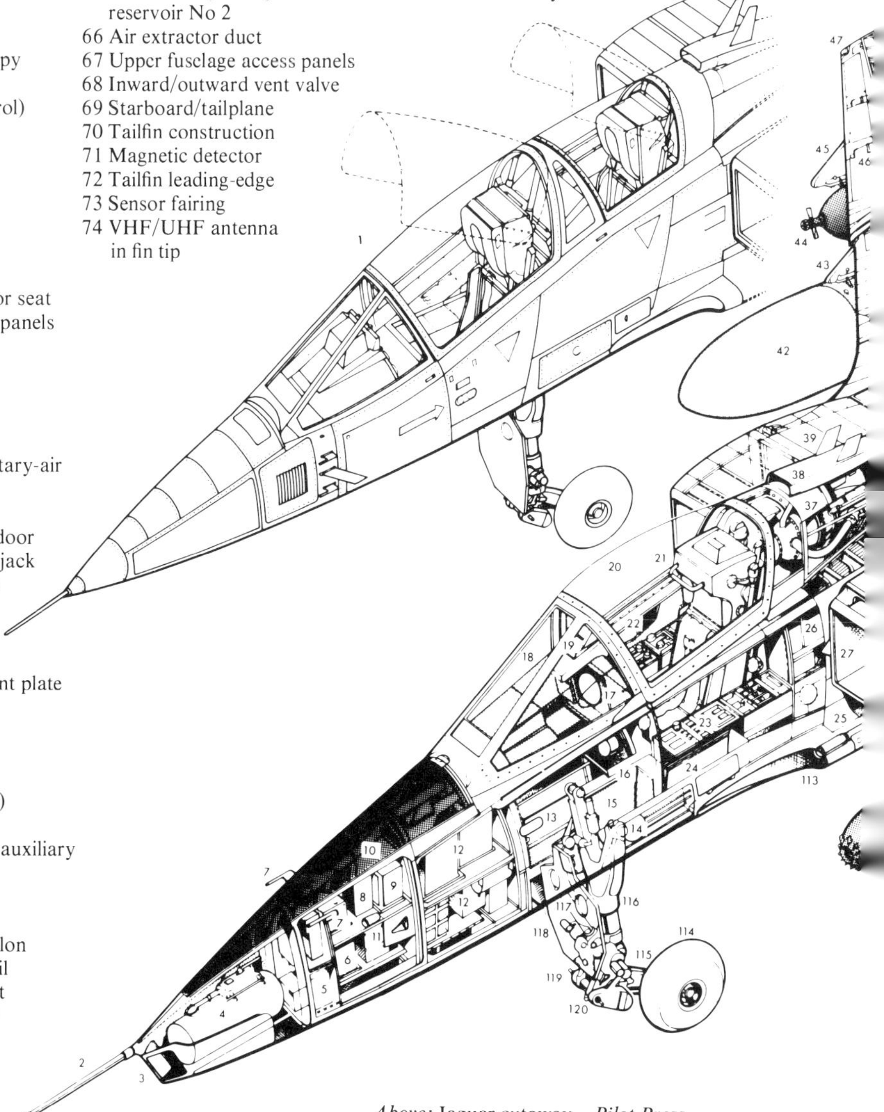

Above: Jaguar cutaway. *Pilot Press*

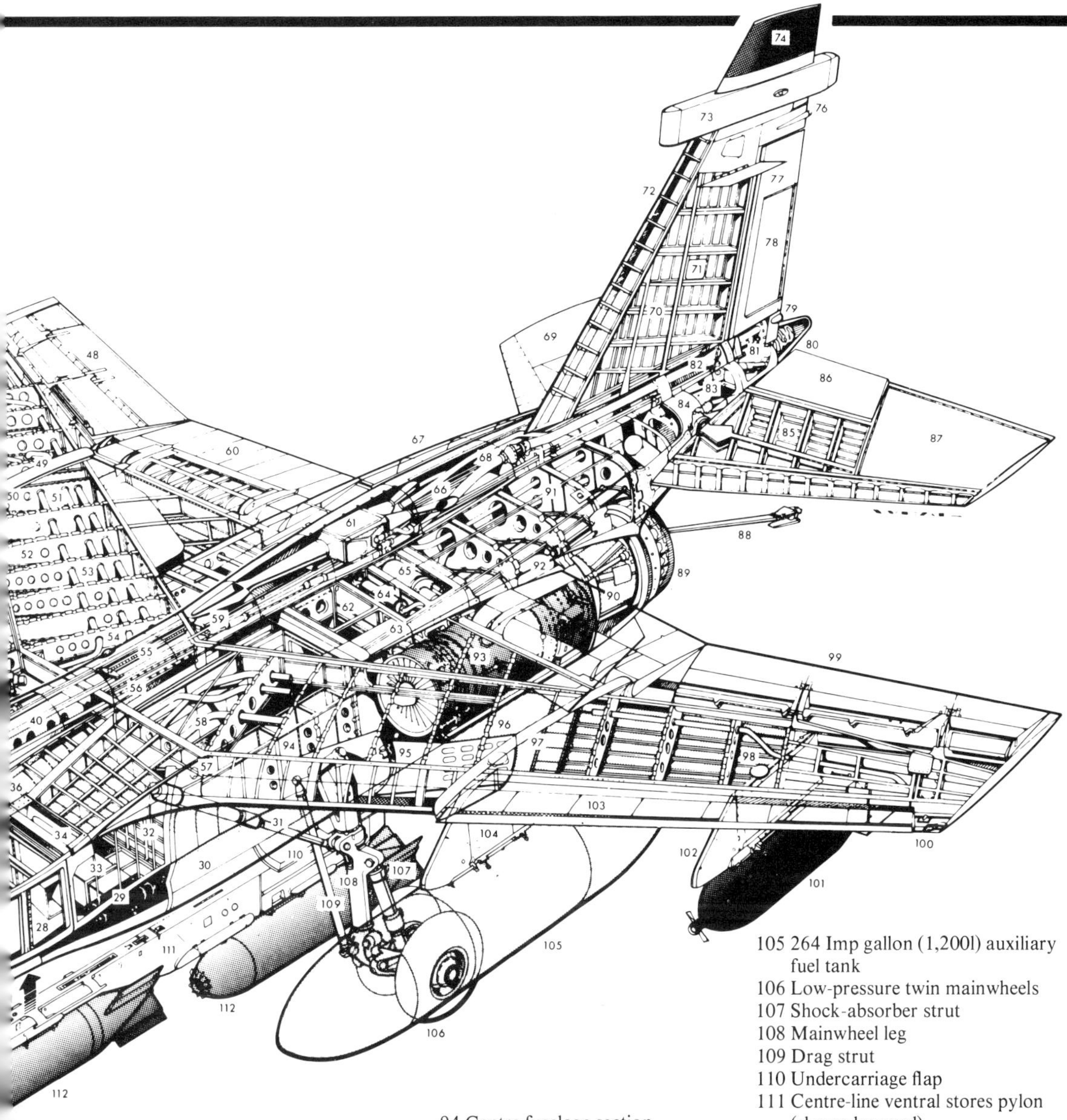

105 264 Imp gallon (1,200l) auxiliary fuel tank
106 Low-pressure twin mainwheels
107 Shock-absorber strut
108 Mainwheel leg
109 Drag strut
110 Undercarriage flap
111 Centre-line ventral stores pylon (shown lowered)
112 Tandem-mounted BL 755 cluster bombs
113 Cannon port
114 Nosewheel
115 Single (starboard) axle fork
116 Nosewheel leg
117 Two landing lights (one 450W; one 250W)
118 Nosewheel door
119 Anti-shimmy gear
120 Towing lug

94 Centre fuselage section
95 Air brake actuator
96 Air brake (extended)
97 Wing fence
98 Pylon mount
99 Full-span trailing-edge double-slotted flaps
100 Port navigation light
101 1,000lb (472kg) bomb
102 Port outer stores pylon
103 Leading-edge slat
104 Port inner stores pylon

87 Honeycomb-filled outer section
88 Arrester hook (extended)
89 Shroud-ring nozzle flaps
90 Afterburner
91 Aft fuselage integral fuel tanks
92 Engine aft mounting point
93 Rolls-Royce/Turboméca Adour 102 engine

6 All Singing, All Dancing

For an aircraft whose original design dates back to the 1960s, Jaguar has remarkably sophisticated all-singing, all-dancing avionics, employing digital computing, which make it well able to survive against modern defences developed in wars which were not even planned when the aircraft was in embryo. Completely different philosophies were employed by the British and French air staffs in drawing up their specifications for the avionics which were to be fitted to their respective Jaguar versions. In the French trainer, the simplest possible system based on a master reference gyro and Tacan receiver was all that was considered necessary, while the French A version was fitted with a system based on equipment which was in service with the French Air Force, consisting of a doppler radar to provide a ground speed and drift angle, an analogue computer to carry out the navigation and weapon-aiming computations, a twin gyro platform, and Tacan.

In the case of the British, the philosophy was to opt for an advanced system based on inertial navigation, and to have the same system fitted in both the trainer and the operational aircraft, so providing dual instruction in all aspects of low-level navigation and low-level weapon delivery — a very demanding task. A major aim of the British system was to provide simplicity of operation for the pilot, leaving him free to concentrate his maximum attention on flying the aircraft — of special value during those parts of the mission where he depends on low altitude flying to avoid detection and achieve surprise. The system gives Jaguar pilots the ability to select and locate their targets without any assistance from the ground. It is possible to make extremely accurate attacks against targets of opportunity as well as pre-planned targets.

In choosing a navigation and attack system for the RAF, the main points which were considered were: that Jaguar would be in service throughout the 1970s and 1980s, so that the system chosen should have the flexibility and capacity to cater for operations under conditions that the designers could not really foresee, using weapons which were only, at that time, in the project stage. It was quickly decided that only digital computing could meet this requirement. Secondly, only an inertial velocity sensor could provide the degree of data to complement the digital computing system. The inertial platform provided a self-contained system, neither transmitting nor receiving signals that might be jammed or otherwise interfered with. Thirdly, it was decided that digital-inertial systems would, with

Left: Pilot's-eye view through the combining glass of the Smiths Industries electronic head-up display in a two-seat Jaguar. *Smiths Industries*

Right: The black boxes which make the Jaguar such a formidable opponent in bad weather conditions are laid out in front of one of the early aircraft. The boxes comprise the Marconi-Elliott NAVWASS-navigation and weapon-aiming system *The Times*

Right: First indication that British Aerospace intended to modify a Jaguar as a fly-by-wire test bed aircraft came with this model slipped on to the company's stand at the 1979 Paris air show. *Brian M. Service*

the high reliability which they were beginning to reach, be more cost-effective than older, but more tried systems.

A further consideration was that range to the target was one of the most important data requirements in an airborne weapons system, the laser rangefinder having a faster response than any other means of deriving air-to-surface, or air-to-air range, performing well at the low grazing angles necessary for modern laydown attacks. The equipment also acted as a target-seeking system when the target was designated by a ground source. An automatic map display became a necessity because the pilot, flying low and fast, had to establish his position relative to the ground without shuffling hand-held maps. The designers also accepted that under battlefield conditions, reference to instruments inside the cockpit is both difficult and dangerous, and this led to a requirement to provide primary flight information within the pilot's field of view — a head-up display. Contracts were let as follows: Marconi-Elliott Avionics Systems, navigation and weapon aiming computer and interface, inertial platform and electronics, projected map display, navigation control unit, weapon aiming mode selector, hand controller, HSI mode selector, and air data computer; Ferranti, laser rangefinder and marked target seeker; Smiths Industries, head-up display, horizontal situation indicator; Sperry Gyroscope Division, gyro-magnetic compass.

Before he enters the aircraft, the pilot checks the weapon load being carried and makes sure that the indicator board situated in the nosewheel bay shows the correct weapons for each station. On entering the cockpit, he confirms that the weapon control panel shows the same information. The Marconi Elliott Avionics Systems E3R inertial platform is started on its alignment cycle by the insertion into the MCS920M digital computer of the present position of the aircraft and the magnetic variation, and by the synchronisation of the Sperry gyro-magnetic compass. All of the systems which have a significant warm-up time are then switched on — IFF, Smiths industries head-up display, Tacan, radio, instrument landing system, and Smiths Industries radar altimeter.

The nav/attack system is then prepared for the sortie. The turning points, predicted wind at sortie height, all target information, and diversion airfields required, and the QDM (Magnetic course to steer) for the ILS at the intended landing field are all inserted into the computer by simple actions on the hand controller in conjunction with the navigation control unit. The pilot then carries out the normal left-to-right cockpit checks, and the engines are started by means of the Micro-Turbo air generator self-starter. When the NAV light on the navigation control unit (NCU) comes on, indicating that the platform is ready, the pilot selects the mode switch from ALIGN to NAV and selects a first destination from one of the turning points already fed into the computer. He then checks that the projected map display (PMD), the horizontal situation indicator (HSI) and the head-up display (HUD) all show the same information in their different ways. The aircraft is then ready for flight.

Pilot read-out in flight is provided by the HUD, which is a complete instrument system in its own right, on which is superimposed a flight director giving steering command, to hold the aircraft on its planned track at any height which the pilot selects. The system is updated occasionally from visual sightings if necessary, and the change destination button is pressed at each turning point. When the aircraft gets to within two minutes of a turning point, on target, the HUD changes from navigation mode to either close navigation, in the case of a turning point, or the first selected attack mode in the case of a target. The flight director on the HUD is replaced by a ground-stabilised marker which physically points out to the

Above: Jaguar T2, XX844/DZ, of No 31 Squadron from RAF Brüggen. *M. Horseman*

Left: A line up of NATO tactical fighters at the Allied Air Forces Central Europe Tactical Air Meet held at RAF Wildenrath in June 1978, and including (nearest the camera) five Jaguar GR1s of No 20 Squadron from RAF Brüggen. *M. Horseman*

Above right: The first Jaguar GR1 delivered to the Royal Air Force was XXIII, seen here at RAF Lossiemouth in June 1974 and carrying the Jaguar Operational Conversion Unit's fin code '01'. Early production aircraft were delivered without the 'chisel nose' configuration, subsequently incorporated as a standard feature to course the laser rangefinder and marked target seeker system, and also absent was the later-fitted mid-fin ECM pod. *M. Horseman*

Right: Jaguar GR1, XX122, of No 54 Squadron seen at the unit's home station, RAF Coltishall, in June 1980. *Denis Calvert/Inter-Air Press*

01

reverts to the navigation mode, and any new destination can then be selected. Targets-of-opportunity attacks are designed to allow the pilot to carry out fully-computed attacks against unplanned targets, without going through the setting-up stages of a planned attack. By selecting the TGT OPP on the WAMS he changes the HUD immediately into an attack mode, and can carry out an attack on an opportunity target without any downgrading of system accuracy if the subsequent ranging and tracking requirements are fulfilled.

Numerous reversionary facilities can be provided within the Jaguar navigation and attack system. For instance, navigation can still be carried out using air data, forecast wind and raw heading information in the event of failure of the inertial sub-system. The reversionary HUD mode gives the pilot a high probability of successfully completing a mission, even with a major system failure present. Provision has been made for the failure of either the inertial velocity sub-system (IVS) or the computing sub-system. In designing these display modes, the prime requirement is to make the pilot aware that a failure of a major unit has occurred, and to ensure that no erroneous information is still displayed. If a failure of either the IVS or the computer occurs during the navigation phase of flight, the HUD will automatically show a breakaway cross, and any erroneous information will be occulted. When a secondary source of information is available, this will then be displayed — C2J Sperry compass when the IVS fails, for instance — and thus the breakaway cross tells the pilot that a failure has occurred.

By inspection, he can then discover which component has failed and he is thereby able to assess the quality of the information which is currently being shown to him. If an equipment failure occurs during a weapon-aiming phase of flight, the HUD will automatically revert to a failed navigation display. The pilot then has the facility of selecting a reversionary weapon-aiming mode. This takes the form of manually-depressable aiming symbol which can be set according to the preferred attack conditions and the weapons being used. By these methods, the pilot has ample facilities for covering major component failures at any stage of his sortie without the end result proving abortive.

When it was introduced into the Jaguar, the Marconi-Elliott navigation and weapons aiming system (NAVWASS) was described by the manufacturers as, 'Europe's most comprehensive' fit of its kind. The basic E3R inertial platform is a fully-manoeuvrable four-gimbal inertial platform using three single degree of freedom gyroscopes and three accelerometers. Information on aircraft acceleration, heading and velocity is passed via the platform electronic unit (PEU) and interface unit (IFU) to the 920M digital computer. The PEU is a hybrid computer which processes the signals from the E3R and provides outputs of velocity and attitude. In addition, it carries out a monitoring function on the correct working of the E3R and its power supplies, as well as controlling the automatic erection sequence and selection of reversionary modes. Conversion of the inputs and outputs of the 920M digital computer is carried out by the interface unit. The forms of signal accepted by the IFU include dc voltages and synchro and digital information. In effect, it is an interpreter between analogue and digital information. In addition to its prime function, the IFU also contains the accurate time reference for the system and provides the power supplies for the 920M and for the navigation control unit (NCU).

The 920M is the central computer for the NAVWASS. It is a 8,912-word store machine with 18 bits a word. Inputs are received from some 14 different sources via the IFU. Elliott 'packaged' the programme in such a way that this small unit is able to perform all the functions which used to be associated with machines of much larger capacity and size. Elliott concluded in designing for the Jaguar that in a single-seater strike aircraft, immediately available information presented in an unambiguous way is of great importance. The NAVWASS includes digital readouts of 20 types of information on the NCU, the PMP, which shows the aircraft's present position, track and direction to selected waypoints, HSI and HUD. The symbols on the Jaguar HUD are the result of many years of work both by the Royal Aircraft Establishment, Farnborough, and Smiths Industries. The display at its simplest form consists of an aircraft symbol, artificial horizon lines, zenith and nadir stars, and a presentation of height, airspeed and heading. In addition to this information, the Jaguar display presents angle of attack, vertical speed, time-to-go, and weapon-aiming information.

Digesting the lessons of the Vietnam and Yom Kippur wars, the French became anxious during the early 1970s to acquire their own stand-off bomb release system for use against heavily-defended targets. But the American systems in use at that time had been developed for use by two-seat strike aircraft, with the observer operating the guidance system and so taking the load from the pilot. Martin Marietta, of Georgia, and the French company Thomson-CSF, cooperated on developing a system which could be operated by the one pilot in the Jaguar without increasing his workload beyond acceptable proportions. The complete system was produced in two parts. The first was ATLIS (automatic tracking laser illumination system). It is housed in a pod carried on Jaguar's centreline pylon and consists of a laser designator and a wide-angle television camera, the field of view of which is centred down the line of the laser beam. The assembly is stabilised and held steady regardless of the movement of the aircraft. The second part of the system consists of a modular laser guidance unit called ARIEL, which is implanted in the nose cone of rockets, missiles or bombs.

Operating ATLIS, the pilot recognises the target and takes a rough line-of-sight through his HUD. He then switches his gaze to the TV monitor and, with the hand controller, makes an accurate fix. He then initiates laser emission to determine the distance to the target, and begins automatic target tracking. Immediately he is within missile range, he launches the weapon which he is carrying and then banks away from the danger area. No matter how violent his evasive manoeuvres might be, the laser beam will remain locked on to the target until the impact is made. After leaving the area, the pilot can continue to make fine adjustments on his monitor, or switch to another target, provided it is in close proximity and visible on his screen. As a safety device, a pitch-and-roll indicator and a dangerous-height warning marker are displayed on the screen to advise the pilot of his aircraft's attitude while he is carrying out head-down, follow-through procedures.

In bad weather conditions, when visibility is poor, the pilot relies on his navigation computer to bring the pod to bear in the vicinity of the target, and then relies on the TV camera. This operates near infra-red in the electromagnetic spectrum, and the enlarged picture on his monitor will display the target still unseen to the naked eye. The system is very flexible, and it is possible for one aircraft to illuminate the target with its ATLIS pod, whilst another aircraft releases its laser-guided weapons. In the case of a mass air attack, when several neighbouring targets such as a squadron of tanks are illuminated at the same time, confusion is avoided by using a code which governs the laser pulse rate to which the associated missile detector is tuned. The weapon will thus only recognise the target designated by its parent launch aircraft.

The French Air Force chose the AS30 air-to-ground laser missile to operate in conjunction with the ATLIS fire-control system. This is supersonic and was developed by Aerospatiale with a Thomson-CSF ARIEL laser auto-director fitted. It is powered by a two-stage solid fuel motor and is controlled by a two-phase guidance system, the first phase being a gyroscopic pre-guidance fit, which initially keeps the missile parallel to the launch axis. The second phase is the terminal guidance system which activates as soon as the laser energy reflected back from the target is sufficiently strong to lock on to the spot illuminated by ATLIS.

The flight path to the target during this second phase is maintained by a system of jet interceptors which are located at the sustaining motor jet outlet. These guidance jets respond to commands from the computer which steer the missile by proportional navigation, from error-detector signals issued by the auto director. On impact, a powerful charge is detonated which is effective against hard targets of concrete and steel. The missile is stored in two sealed containers and requires only periodic inspection. When required, it can be fitted quickly under the aircraft wing with a minimum of final safety checks. It has a range of 6.2 miles.

On 21 October 1981 the Jaguar fly-by-wire had its first flight from BAe Warton's aerodrome in Lancashire — the world's first aircraft to fly solely with an all-digital quadruplex fly-by-wire control system. Apart from considerable weight savings the main advantage of ACT (Active Control Technology) is that an unstable aircraft can now be flown.
Below: Take-off of XX765 flown by BAe Warton's Senior Experimental Test Pilot Chris Yeo. *BAe*

Left: Jaguar GR1, XZ113, of No 41 Squadron. *R. J. Wilson*

Right: The powerful lines of the Jaguars are in evidence in this close-up of XX721, a two-seater somewhere off the coast of Britain. *Image in Industry*

Below: A Jaguar flight line at RAF Lossiemouth in June 1974; the nearest aircraft, XX726, was the first issued to No 6 Squadron and also the first to be delivered with the full production standard 'chisel nose'. *M. Horseman*

XX721

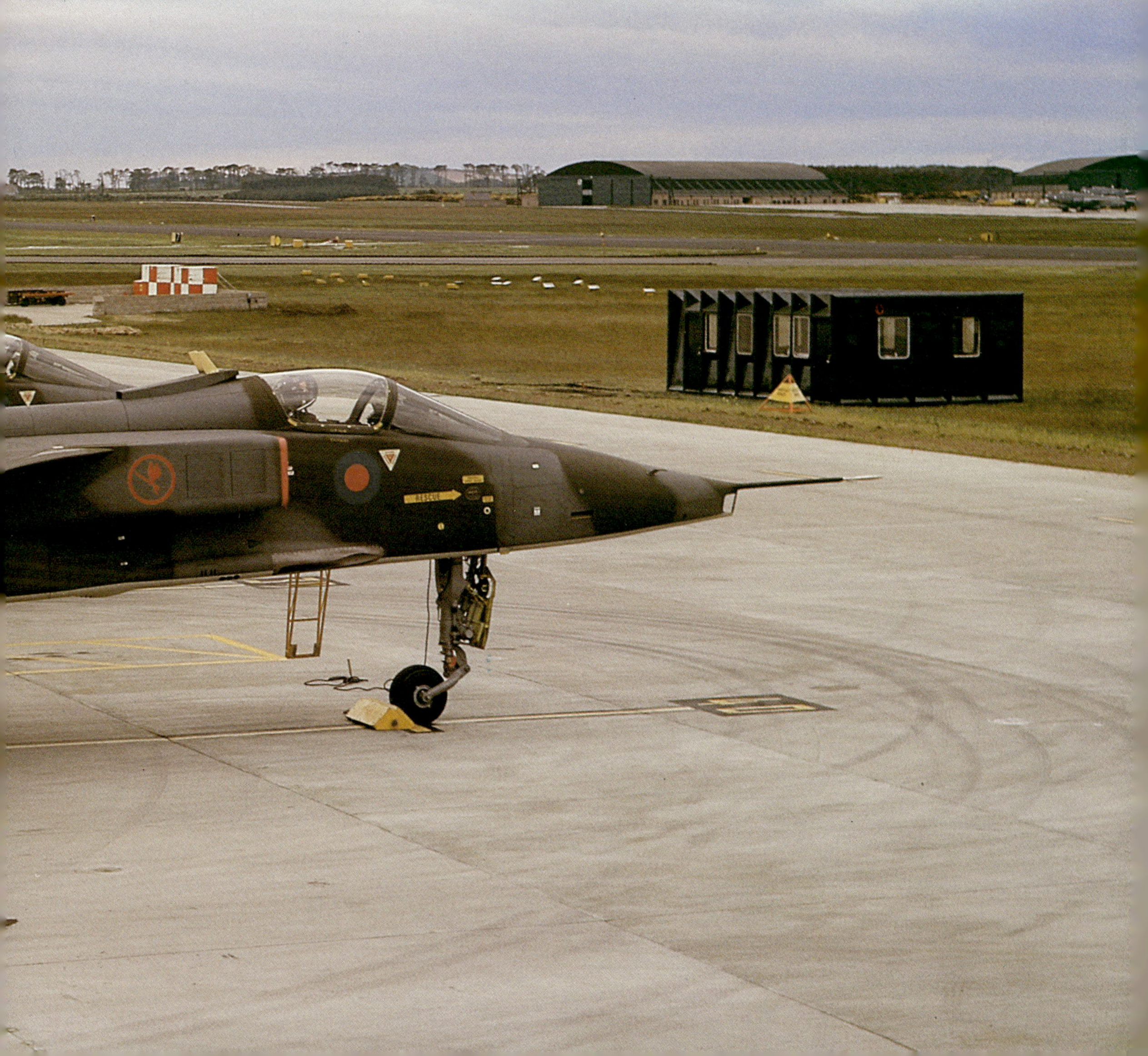
RESCUE

7 Into French Service

Aircraft deliveries to the French Air Force began on 4 May 1972 when the first production machine arrived from the final assembly line at the Mont-de-Marsan air base, near Bordeaux. Training of pilots and mechanics began there in preparation for the formation of the first operational unit at St Dizier in north-eastern France — a moment which was officially marked on 19 June 1973 with ceremonies attended by the Minister for the Armed Forces, M Robert Galley, and the Chief of the French Air Staff, General Claude Grigaut.

General Grigaut took that opportunity to review the progress of the project which, he said, was a 'product of French-British tenacity', and which had had, 'a certain number of detractors'. The project had required much perseverance and much faith. 'For the first time,' the general went on, 'the French Air Force has an excellent support aircraft that meets all criteria demanded by this role, both conventional and nuclear. It can defend itself, has inflight refuelling capability, can operate from short runways, and constitutes a particularly stable weapons platform'. Jaguar, he was convinced, 'would last a score of years'.

This was the first time on which it had been officially confirmed that Jaguar was to be used to carry France's tactical nuclear bomb, the AN52, and that its operational roles included that of supplementing the Mirage IV on low-level penetration missions. The French single-seat A version would, it became clear, be used for the following missions: close support, with eight 880lb bombs, 11×550lb bombs, or 15×275lb bombs; air superiority at low or medium altitude with Matra Magic air-to-air missiles; reconnaissance, with fixed provision for the OMERA 40 panoramic camera; low-altitude penetration, with AS37 Martel anti-radar missiles and two external 264gal fuel tanks; and, intervention overseas, with three external tanks and in-flight refuelling giving a range of 2,485 miles and an endurance of 10 hours.

The 7th *Escadre de Chasse*, then located at Nancy-Ochey with two *escadrons*, the 1/7 Provence and the

Below left: Framed by anti-aircraft guns, a Jaguar prototype stands between two FAF aircraft. The Jaguars had just been delivered to the St Dizier base, and aircrew (left) discuss their new charges. *Image in Industry*

Below: Casque de Bayard squadron crews of the FAF on the flight line at St Dizier with their Jaguars. *BAe*

Below right: Impressive line-up of weaponry as the first French Air Force Jaguar squadron commissions in June 1973. *Image in Industry*

3/7 Languedoc had been selected by the *Armée de l'Air* as long ago as 1968 to be its first Jaguar unit. They were then flying Mystere IVs, described by their pilots as, '*un avion simple et rustique*', so that the conversion to sophisticated Jaguar must have come as a relief. But such a jump in equipment also brought retraining problems, and these were made worse by the fact that the unit moved its base from Nancy to St Dizier before receiving its new aircraft. *Escadron* 1/7 was the first to convert, 3/7 following by the end of 1973. The 11th *Escadre de Chasse*, based at Toul-Rosieres, and then equipped with outmoded North American F-100 Super Sabres, began to convert to the Jaguar in 1974.

By the end of 1973, the FAF had received 28 aircraft and was planning for an intake of 28-30 annually over the next three years. Of the first ten Jaguars delivered, five Es and two As were assigned to the CEAM at Mont-de-Marsan whose task is similar to that of Boscombe Down, that is, to draw up the operational guidelines for the squadrons. By the middle of 1973, total Jaguar production was building up to eight a month. Five of these were going to the RAF, whose need for a new tactical strike aircraft was, it had been agreed between the two partner governments, more vital at that time than that of the French. At the formal ceremonies at St Dizier in June, General Grigaut gave his impressions of flying the Jaguar. He had had, he said, 'a comfortable feeling' in the cockpit, as a result of flying an impressive aircraft at low level. 'Between ground level and 25,000ft it is highly manoeuvrable, including along the longitudinal axis. Acceleration and deceleration is remarkable, and its steadiness cannot be faulted. The aircraft has its own characteristics which the pilot has to get used to. For example, flying the approach at constant incidence, while it is not completely novel, has to be practised. However, it should not cause any difficulties. Besides its flying characteristics, this aircraft must be given high marks for the comfort of its cockpit, and its good visibility. As a pilot, I have a high opinion of the Jaguar.'

Early shortages of spares proved a worry, as was hinted by one of the first FAF officers to convert. 'As far as the ground crews are concerned, they consider the availability of the aircraft is directly connected to the provisioning of the spares. The provisioning programme which has been set up within the project calls for international cooperation. A computerised system for spares provision has been set up recently within the FAF. These factors contribute to the complication of a system, which although it will probably be satisfactory in the future, is unwieldy at present.'

By July 1975, two years later, Jaguars had flown a total of 30,000 hours (5,000 hours in development and trials, 13,000 hours with the FAF, and 12,000 hours with the RAF). The first two FAF squadrons were reporting an improvement of 30% in air-to-ground gun firing results compared with anything else it had in its armoury. All the other weapons had been cleared by that time, except for the Magic missile, trials of which began towards the end of 1975. A spectacular salvo of four canisters of 36 rockets each was fired from aircraft E01 as part of these trials without, it was found,

A French Air Force Jaguar, A22 of EC1/7 'Provence', showing the port side fin insignia of SPA15, June 1974.
M. Horseman

A two-seat and a single-seat of the Omani Air Force lift off in formation from a desert runway. *BAe*

Above: Three French Air Force Jaguars low down in formation approach a typical coastline in northern France.
Dassault-Breguet via Mike Hooks

Right: French Air Force Jaguar fires an AS30 laser-guided missile from a rail under the starboard wing. The aircraft carries an Atlis 11 pod under the fuselage.
Gifas via Mike Hooks

Below right: Under-fuselage fuel tank on this two-seat Jaguar carries the Agave radar in its nose. *BAe*

The conversion of the ground enginee
Jaguar was not such a happy story, howe
took about six months, but the numbers e
or fully trained were very far below the de
scheduled in the established list. It
however, that Jaguar, although a new
therefore creating new problems, requi
men to service it than did the older, less
types which it was replacing. 2/7 was
monthly average of hours flown of 280-3(
tructors were converting up to six pilots
Seventeen aircraft were in use, of which
seats.

Above: Close-up of the fin and tailplane of a French Air Force Jaguar. The insignia is the archer of 2/7 squadron. *Dassault-Breguet*

producing any aerodynamic effect on the control surfaces. All of the A versions starting with the 80th off the assembly line were fitted with the laser range finder.

The 7th *Escadre de Chasse* was fully operational on the Jaguar with three squadrons, 1/7 with a nuclear role, 2/7 Argonne with a peacetime training role and a wartime role of low and medium cover and tactical support of ground forces, and 3/7 also in the nuclear role. The pilot conversion cycle in the FAF was, two weeks on the ground with 16 simulator sessions followed by flight conversion consisting of 40 missions over two months for young pilots, or 15 missions over one month for pilots already trained, or 10 missions for pilots with at least 1,500 hours in their log book. First flight was always in the rear seat of the trainer with a brief to watch and do nothing else. Then followed three familiarisation flights each lasting over an hour including navigation, blind flying, and air-to-ground gun firing, with the young pilot being allowed to go solo after 10 flights.

Right: Early French Air Force two-seat Jaguars on the flight line of the FAF base at St Dizier. *Dassault-Breguet*

Below right: Jaguars of the *Casque de Bayard* squadron of the FAF in immaculate line. The lead aircraft has the squadron flag mounted on the cockpit rim. *Image in Industry*

Banking away from the chase aircraft, the pilot of the early Jaguar International displays a selection of stores and the special badge designed for this uprated version. This incorporates the French and British flags but in fact Dassault did little to promote International sales. *BAe*

which caused many an argument in messes on either side of the Channel was the wide divergence in simulator techniques, with the RAF criticising the French version for being too simple, and the FAF in turn saying that that used by the RAF was far too sophisticated. Availability of the Jaguar in the early French squadrons was remarkably high, with 90% recorded during a particularly demanding exercise where 12 aircraft were committed over 12 days.

By 1978, the FAF had firmed up on nine squadrons of Jaguars, each of 15 aircraft, giving 130 in all. But as France had ordered a total of 200, what was to happen to the remainder? General Philippe Fleurot, Commander of the FAF Tactical Air Command, said that contrary to former practice of sending supplementary aircraft out to operational units, they would be cocooned at the Chateaudun Centre. Stored this way the aircraft would be prevented from ageing, 'and economies are made in maintenance'. The general added, 'they can, of course, be put into service in a very short space of time. They will be kept in reserve, since it is visualised that Jaguars will have an important role to play in the 1990s'. The RAF and the FAF, the general also confirmed, were working closely together in the exchange of information concerning flight safety and tactics.

The 11th Wing of the FAF received its full complement of Jaguars by July 1977, in three squadrons, 1/11 Roussillon, 2/11 Vosges and 3/11 Corse. The principal mission of 1/11 was conventional attack in support of the French 1st Army. Experience had shown that a load in this role of bombs and ventral tanks, as well as the two 30mm cannon, was a good compromise between radius of action and payload. 2/11's principal mission was to study and define the best tactical use of electronic warfare equipment with the wartime task of confusing enemy surveillance radar and creating gaps in the screen through which accompanying aircraft could penetrate. 3/11's main task was the support of French interests overseas. Its complement included eight two-seats to enable constant instruction in flight refuelling. Each pilot had an average of three such flights a month.

One criticism which was being heard in the FAF at this time was that the French E version was not an exact replica in its equipment of the single-seat A version, being far less sophisticated. The RAF two-seat B version did not suffer from this drawback, it was pointed out, and with the exception of having only one cannon and no in-flight refuelling capability, was equipped to exactly the same standards as the single-

Left: French Air Force two-seat Jaguar poses close-up for the camera. *Dassault-Breguet*

seat S version, thus having virtually the same combat capability.

One squadron of the 3rd Fighter Wing, the 3/3 Ardennes, was equipped with Jaguars, the other two squadrons, 1/3 Navarre, and 2/3 Champagne keeping their Mirage IIIs. The principal mission given to the 3/3 aircraft was a common one for the whole wing, to assist penetration of defences using the Martel anti-radar missile. By the end of the 1970s, the Belouga dispenser pod was also in wide use as a ground-attack weapon by the FAF. Based on the British BL755 cluster bomb developed by Hunting Engineering, and in use by RAF Jaguar squadrons, each Belouga casing contained 151 small grenades. After release, the weapon was braked to enable the Jaguar to clear the area before the grenades ejected at a regular rate, forming a ground pattern. The grenades were also individually braked so that they hit the ground in an almost vertical position for maximum effect.

Right: Four French Air Force single-seater Jaguars keep close station in staggered line-abreast on the camera plane. *Dassault-Breguet*

Below: An early FAF single-seater taxies in a sylvan setting towards the end of the runway. Makers' name is still on the nose and serial number on the fin. *Dassault-Breguet*

Above: Three of the early development aircraft, two-seaters nearest and furthest from the camera, and a single-seat in the lead in FAF camouflage. *Dassault-Breguet*

Left: Prototype 03 out on a test flight and wearing French Air Force paint and insignia shows its clean lines unencumbered by any stores or rails. *Dassault-Breguet*

Below left: A French Air Force two-seater lets go its tail braking parachute as its main wheels touch the runway. *Dassault-Breguet*

Three types of grenade were developed — general purpose fragmentation for use against vehicle convoys, equipment, fuel stores and parked aircraft; armour-piercing for use against tanks and other hard-skinned vehicles; and area interdiction for use against airfields, harbours and railway yards. The Belouga could be released at speeds of up to 500mph with the Jaguar flying as low as 120ft, and the pilot could select one of two ground patterns before release. A typical FAF Jaguar Belouga stores load would be nine canisters, three each on two underwing positions and three on a centreline rail, plus a pair of Matra Magic missiles for dogfighting on outboard underwing stations.

The Magic was tasked by the FAF for close-in air-to-air combat, with an effective range shorter even than the 500yd of the cannon, although this was considerably extended at high altitude. Magic could be fired in very tight turns and could withstand lateral acceleration up to 50g, allowing it to be fired from abeam of the target. It had an infra red homing device, and its frequency band was selected to make it extremely sensitive to the emission of carbon dioxide gases, in addition to the infra red radiation from hot engine gases. During FAF trials, Magic was successfully fired from underwing rails on the Jaguar. The overwing mounting, which was proved in firing trials from Warton, was considered to be the logically-correct one for the majority of combat situations because, when the aircraft was pulling round towards its target, the missiles were looking upwards from the wing and into the turn. In the trials it was found that the missiles left their launcher rails cleanly and that their efflux was well clear of the Jaguar engine intakes.

Above and left: Close-ups of the M05 maritime prototype show the unique single wheels main undercarriage of this one-off aircraft and the radar nose. *Breguet*

Right: The maritime, or M, prototype of the Jaguar, for the French Navy, underwent deck landing trials at Bedford. It is seen here on the RAE deck, carrying a selection of stores, and in a clean configuration being pulled to a quick stop by its tail parachute. *Dassault-Breguet*

Above: Twelve take-offs and landings were made from the *Clemenceau* during deck trials in 1971. Here M05 comes in for a touchdown. The main external difference between the maritime version and land-based version is clear in this picture — single main wheels instead of pairs, and twin nosewheel, instead of a single wheel. *Dassault-Breguet*

Right: A series of test flights from the French aircraft carrier *Clemenceau* off Lorient in October 1971, proved the suitability of the maritime version of the Jaguar for that type of operation. But the version was later cancelled, and the French bought the Super Etendard instead. *Dassault-Breguet*

Below right: Netted. The M05 maritime prototype pictured through the arrester gear during its deck landing trials at RAE Bedford in 1971 *BAe*

8 A High Performance Little Ship

Regular deliveries of production Jaguars to the RAF conversion unit at Lossiemouth began on 13 September 1973 with the arrival from Warton of single-seaters S7 and S8 (although S4 had been delivered there in May of the same year for ground-crew training). The pilots on 13 September were, Sqn Ldr John Preece, and Jerry Lee, a BAC test pilot. The deliveries followed a conversion course at Warton for pilots lasting two weeks. They were led by Wing Commander John Walker, then officer commanding the Jaguar conversion team at Lossiemouth. Conversion to type was the responsibility of BAC test pilots.

On 5 June the following year, 1974, Jaguar officially entered squadron service with the RAF with No 54 in a ceremony at Lossiemouth. Lined up on that occasion were 14 of the new aircraft, including two visiting French Air Force Jaguars, and one in the colours of No 6, the second Jaguar squadron to be formed. The No 6 Squadron aircraft was equipped with the laser nose, the first time that the device had been displayed in public. No 54 Squadron, it was announced, was to deploy later in 1974 to RAF Coltishall, Norfolk, which was to become the permanent base for Jaguar in the UK. It was to be followed to Coltishall by No 6 after it had converted and worked up at Lossiemouth.

Air Chief Marshal Sir Denis Smallwood, Air Officer Commanding-in-Chief, Strike Command, at that time, outlined the Service's plans for its new bird. Later in 1974, the emphasis of the training at Lossiemouth would change to the formation of further squadrons which would move to RAF Germany. The UK's requirements would be completed in about 1976. Five Jaguar squadrons would be based in Germany as part of the Second Allied Tactical Air Force under the Supreme Allied Commander Europe (SACEUR). They would be concerned with fulfilling the roles of interdiction, battlefield support and reconnaissance. Three UK-based squadrons would form part of the Mobile Force in conjunction with the Third Division of the British Army.

Wg Cdr Walker took the opportunity at the ceremony to praise both the design and performance of the Jaguar. 'The object of the exercise,' he said, 'is to put the bomb on the target, and that is what the Jaguar does better than anything else we have. Jaguar

Right: Squashed Jaguar. A taxying aircraft provided this unusual shot for Harry Kerr in an airfield mirror landing aid. *Harry Kerr, The Times*

Below: Two Lossiemouth Jaguars make a landing approach. The two-seat on the left is in the clean configuration, while the single-seater has a fuel tank on the centreline and practice bomb carriers on the outboard wing stations. *Harry Kerr, The Times*

Top: The RAF's first Jaguar soon after arrival at RAF Lossiemouth at the end of May, 1973. It was flown there by Squadron Leader John Preece and greeted on arrival by Gp Capt Michael Robinson, station commander.
Harry Kerr, The Times

Above: Jaguar line up at Lossiemouth in the summer of 1974. *The Times*

Left: A Lossiemouth two-seater is hauled to a short stop through the use of its tail parachute.
Harry Kerr, The Times

is a very high-performance little ship to the extent that it surprises Lightning pilots. Operationally, it is very, very hard to stop it. Jaguar will hit the target. We will take on any other unit in the RAF on low-level, high-speed bomb dropping and we will outbomb them — and this is with an aircraft which has been in service for about eight months.' He illustrated the accuracy of the navigation and weapon-aiming system by recalling an instance during an early training mission. 'We came below cloud over the target area, but we couldn't see the target at first because we had the target marker cross on the head-up display turned up too bright and right over the actual target. That really impressed us from the outset.'

Above: Adjacent photography; Jaguar two-seat recycles its undercarriage right up in the lens of the camera (the tail of the photo aircraft can be seen in the top left corner).
Brian M. Service

On cockpit layout, the wing commander had this to say, 'The designers got the priorities right. Everything that matters is right in front of you. The pilots like the cockpit. It is a very, very good fighter cockpit'. On survivability: 'We haven't yet been shot at, but with a lot of fuel in a small aircraft, it would take a very serious and lucky hit to take you completely out of fuel. Like the Americans found in Vietnam, operationally the twin-engined aircraft really comes into its own. The great survivability factor, we feel, is that for the first time really we have got an aircraft where you can virtually guarantee — on interdiction-type targets — making the very fast, low-level straight pass attack. This must surely be one of the big aids in keeping yourself in one piece.' On range: 'Jaguar carries as much internal fuel as the Hunter has with both internal and external fuel tanks, which gives it a very impressive range without external drop tanks. We can carry three 265 gallon external fuel tanks, but have not yet had cause to go that far. Normally, we operate with two tanks. We have had two hours 25 minutes missions flown by the OCU here. This is a very long-range aircraft.'

On reliability: 'I don't think we have had an aircraft into service, certainly in my timescale, that has had a record such as the Jaguar. We have flown over 1,500 hours with only one instance of an electrical failure in the air. That was the loss of one of two alternators and the other can take the whole load. Reliability is so good, in fact, that we are having to introduce special emergency training programmes. We are simply not getting emergencies.'

On airfield performance: 'About one and a half times the weight of a Hunter, Jaguar can land slower than a Hunter. It is quite capable of operating from typical flying club-type grass strips. The brake parachute really does pull you up. With a lot of low-pressure rubber on the runway, and high energy — absorbing brakes, the aircraft can pull up very quickly indeed. The big low-pressure tyres and high energy-absorbing undercarriage means you can touch down Jaguar without knowing you have touched. Nosewheel steering means you can use all the brakes in a cross wind.' Maintainability: 'Excellent. The aircraft was laid down from the start with front-line maintenance in mind. My problem this morning is that I don't have enough space to put all my serviceable aircraft out.'

Nav/attack system: 'Built round a digital computer, which is where we think we are picking up the great advantages in weapons delivery accuracy. The navigation accuracy is very much up to specification in

Above: Taking part in the flying display at the 1974 Farnborough air show, a Jaguar two-seat displays its clean planform. *Brian M. Service*

Left: Jaguar two-seat crackles the eardrums in a sprightly take-off during the 1972 Farnborough show.
Brian M. Service

Left: Jaguar tucks its wheels away immediately after take-off from the Farnborough show, 1974. *Brian M. Service*

Below: An impressive line up of Jaguars at RAF Lossiemouth. The aircraft nearest the camera bears the insignia of No 6 Squadron. *BAe*

Right: A superb shot taken through the windscreen of a two-seater showing Jaguars out of Lossiemouth banking over the Scottish countryside. *Image in Industry*

service.' Electrical system: 'I think it should be a model for future aircraft design. It is very good indeed in terms of redundancy. You can lose massive parts of the electrical system, and you are still operationally viable.' Weapon load: 'Jaguar can carry 10,000lb of weapons and will eventually be cleared for the full range of French and RAF stores.' Fatigue-life handling: 'Jaguar has a long fatigue life. It was laid down on the drawing board from the start with the low-level environment in mind, and it also handles beautifully at low level.' Wg Cdr Walker summed up, 'Jaguar is possibly the finest pilot's aircraft that many of us have flown. We have had on the OCU staff, and indeed on the courses going through, quite a lot of Hunter pilots. I think you are aware what pilots think of the Hunter — God's gift to fighter aviation in its time. When Hunter pilots say that the Jaguar is an excellent aircraft, that is praise indeed. I think that it is the natural follow-on to the sequence of single-engined fighter aircraft.'

No 54 Squadron declared itself 'combat ready' by the spring of 1975, within a year of forming — and in line with targets set in 1972. By spring 1975, both Nos 54 and 6 were putting eight or nine aircaft out of 10 on the flight lines at Coltishall each day, a testimonial to the maintainability of the RAF's new steed. The first overseas pilots to convert to Jaguar passed through at this time. They were, Capt Ed Cubleigh, of the USAF, and Capt Odd Sandvik, of the Royal Norwegian Air Force. By the spring of 1975, the first Jaguar squadrons were beginning to form at Brüggen, Germany. The first to be based there was No 14, with No 17 re-equipping with Jaguars later the same year. No 31 followed in the early part of 1976.

The first flight simulator for Jaguar was introduced into service at RAF Wildenrath, Germany, and was used initially to train aircrew from Lossiemouth. Lossiemouth followed with its own simulator, when the one at Wildenrath was assigned to the training of crews serving with Jaguar squadrons in Germany. RAF Coltishall brought its simulator into use in October, 1975. The Wildenrath simulator building was divided into four sections containing, the simulator cockpit area, the control and instructions room, the

computer room, and the model room. The platform on which the cockpit was mounted moved in all directions and accurately simulated such movements as taxying across tarmac and concrete, landing and take off, and all conditions of flight, including high-speed turbulence, deceleration and acceleration.

Flight trials of a specially-designed reconnaissance pod for Jaguar were carried out in the spring of 1975 with a view to entering service with the RAF in the spring of 1976. An urgency for this piece of equipment had been underlined by the recent war in the Middle East between Israel and Egypt which had shown that to avoid destruction, attacking aircraft had to fly ever lower and faster, with consequent additional demands on both pilot and equipment. The Hawker Siddeley Dynamics (now BAe) infra-red linescan (IRLS) in the pod enabled Jaguar to step up its low-level reconnaissance missions to speeds approaching Mach 1 at heights well below radar cover. The IRLS was fed with all the relevant information stored in the NAVWASS digital computer, including height, latitude and longitude and aircraft attitude. Roll stabilisation was incorporated to permit high angles of bank without loss of continuity. Distortion of the linescan record from gusts was effectively reduced by roll stabilisation. The aircraft position was printed on every frame, and a facility was incorporated which enabled the pilot to mark an area of particular interest for future reference. This enabled targets to be identified easily and, on subsequent missions, located and attacked with pin-point accuracy.

Production of the pod was at the BAC Weybridge factory. It was carried beneath the centreline of the aircraft, attached by two ejector release units and linked through electrical and pipe connections for air conditioning. IRLS was carried in the rear of the pod, the

Top left: RAF two-seater poses against a backdrop of waves and beaches. *Image in Industry*

Above left: Four Jaguars from No 6 Squadron RAF, each carrying long-range tanks, in tight box formation over the Farnborough air show crowds. *Image in Industry*

Left: Wg Cdr R. J. Kemball, commanding No 54 Squadron RAF, was at the controls of this GR1 out of Coltishall hauling four 1,000lb bombs and two fuel tanks. *BAe*

Above: The first reconnaissance Jaguar, XZ101, to be issued to the first reconnaissance squadron in the RAF is taken on its maiden mission by the commander of No 2 (AC) Squadron, Wg Cdr R. A. F. Wilson. The reconnaissance pod beneath the centreline has roll stabilisation, infra red linescan and forward-looking and fan F95 cameras. Each photographic frame is marked with latitude and longitude from the navigation and weapons aiming sub-system *BAe*

Right: The S1 development Jaguar for the RAF takes off loaded with underwing tanks on the inboard pylons and practice bomb carriers (CBLS100) beneath the fuselage. *BAe*

Above: S06, in RAF markings and camouflage, lines up at the beginning of a test sortie. *BAe*

front and centre being given over to cameras giving horizon-to-horizon cover. The data conversion unit was sited in the rear half. Cameras were installed in two rotatable drums, the rear one carrying alternative modules to enable the complete pod to be covered from low to medium-altitude operations. In the operating position, the cameras viewed the ground through optically-ground glass windows. For low-level sorties, the rear camera drum contained two high oblique across track Vinten F95 Mark 10 cameras with 3in F2 lenses. The alternative module for medium-altitude reconnaissance housed a F126 camera with a 6in F5.6 lens.

The front rotating camera drum, which was common for low and medium-altitude missions, contained two low-oblique across track F95 Mark 10 cameras with 1.5in F2.8 lenses, and one forward-looking oblique F95 Mark 7 camera with 6in F28 lens. Attaching the pod to the Jaguar was a quick and simple procedure with the aid of a special ground-handling trolley. The air pipe connection engaged automatically, while convenient access was provided for the electrical connections, and to enable film to be changed while the pod remained on the aircraft.

Two Jaguar squadrons, No 11 (AC), and No 41, were given the primary task of air photographic reconnaissance, the former forming at Laarbrüch, near the Dutch border in Germany, in 1976, and replacing Phantoms, the latter at Coltishall. A photographic sortie in a Jaguar was very similar to a strike attack sortie, way points and picture targets being fed into the aircraft's computer before take-off. Apart from an occasional glance to compare the projected map display with actual ground position, and if necessary to carry out simple update procedures, the whole sortie was flown by reference to the head-up display, allowing continuous monitoring of the world outside the cockpit and an unencumbered search for likely targets.

After the instructions on the HUD were followed to put the Jaguar on its exact course, the pilot switched on the cameras, an action which rotated them in their protective housing to their predetermined position for photography. All cameras were then selected so that the complete range of view from port to starboard beneath the pod could be recorded instantly by pressing the button mounted on the control column. At precisely two minutes to go before reaching the first target, the HUD changed from a full navigation mode to close navigation, presenting more specialised information for visual acquisition of the target. The flight director was replaced by a ground-stabilised target acquisition marker, and a 'time-to-go' circle. By reference to the acquisition marker, the pilot could easily identify his target and could arrange his flight

Left: Single-seater Jaguars fly in close formation out of their base at RAF Lossiemouth.
Image in Industry

Below: RAF two-seater edges up to the camera, its air brakes extended, during a training sortie. *Monitor*

Above: This unusual plan view gives a good impression of the overwing mounting of the Matra Magic dogfight missiles on a single-seat Jaguar in RAF colours. *BAe*

path to fly over, or to either side of the target to obtain maximum photographic effect. The photographs were taken in a second. The pilot then punched the change destination button, the HUD issued fresh instructions, and the Jaguar was on its way to the next way point.

A further lesson learned from the Arab-Israeli war was that concrete runways become an early target, and with this is mind, Jaguars were involved in two types of trials in the mid-1970s as the RAF consolidated the aircraft in squadron service. In the first of these, Tim Ferguson, BAC military aircraft deputy chief pilot, landed a GR Mk 1 on a stretch of the new M55 motorway near Blackpool, Lancashire. Approach to the landing site involved flying over a bridge carrying a country road across the motorway. The landing run, using the brake parachute, was only 450yd. Turnround on the motorway included fitting four cluster bombs on the wing pylons in addition to a 1,200-litre fuel tank beneath the fuselage. Take-off run began beneath the road bridge, and the aircraft was airborne in about 600yd.

Jaguar's light footprint resulting from its tall undercarriage and twin low-pressure tyres (which complete well over 100 landings in normal conditions) caused no damage to the motorway surface. Ferguson said later, 'Landing the Jaguar on a motorway presented no problems beyond the capability of a squadron pilot, providing he has done a few practice short landings.

Below: Photographic Jaguar for the RAF looks overloaded with its bulbous recce pod and long-range tanks, but still makes a sprightly departure off the runway. *BAe*

We've not done anything new. The landing technique employed is laid down as standard procedure in the pilots' notes for short landing, involving a high-incidence approach and steep glide slope. The secret is to get the touch-down right. Once the wheels are on the ground, the Jaguar's nosewheel steering gives very precise control. In practice on the airfield we had no difficulty in steering the aircraft at over 100kts on a curve similar to the motorway overshoot. Take-off was absolutely straightforward. It's easier than landing. I used the standard short-field take-off technique, and was airborne with plenty to spare in the planned distance'. Using the experience gained from the Ferguson experiment, four Jaguars of No 31 squadron from RAF Brüggen practised emergency landings and take-offs on part of a new autobahn connecting Bremen and Bremerhaven during September 1977.

The second series of trials proved Jaguar's ability to operate out of rough fields and were carried out at the Aeroplane and Armament Establishment (A&AEE), Boscombe Down, in the autumn of 1977. Both single and two-seat versions were involved. The trials strip crossed a runway, an airfield road, two taxiways and two repair mats, and was punctuated with obstacles such as manhole covers, rabbit burrows, shallow ditches and natural indulations. The pilots apparently quickly adjusted to the unaccustomed pitching and cobblestone effects caused by these changes in surface during take-off, landing and taxying over a 'cross-country course'. The sensations experienced were described as being like 'a well-sprung limousine with four-wheel drive'. As a result, the manufacturers concluded that Jaguar had an operational flexibility matched only by V/STOL aircraft, allowing dispersal on airfields closed to all but the lightest machines, while at main bases, operations could continue despite repeated enemy attacks which destroyed main runways and taxiways.

One problem which bugged the aircraft in these early days in service was the low quality of radio transmissions received from Jaguars. This was often blamed on the V/UHF radios installed, but opinion on the squadrons took account of several other factors. The Jaguar cockpit was noisier than some others, which obliged pilots to shout into their microphones in an effort to overcome the background noise. When coupled with two-stage amplification from an aerial

Below: A box of four RAF Jaguars carries an assortment of stores including, on the aircraft nearest the camera, a reconnaissance pod. *BAe*

Above: Symbolic fly-past features one aircraft from each of the five RAF squadrons operating the type in Germany, front to rear, No 2 (reconnaissance), 14, 17, 20 and 31. *BAe*

which was considered less than perfect, some signal distortion was almost inevitable. Transmissions between Jaguars operating in close formation, especially lo-lo between hills, could be particularly hard to make out.

Special flights of pairs of Jaguars were carried out at Warton with the express purpose of improving radio communications. During other trials at Warton, in 1980, Jaguar was fully cleared for target banner towing so that each squadron is now autonomous in air-to-air armament practice. Squadron Jaguars can readily be adapted to 'carry the banner' without calling on specialised target-towing aircraft types.

Jaguar's precision soon began to put it among the competitive honours. No 14 Squadron won the annual RAF Germany navigation and bombing competition for the much-prized Salmond Trophy in both 1975 and 1976, with No 17 Squadron coming second. They were up against Harriers, Buccaneers and Phantoms, and in 1976 nine squadrons took part. Each sortie began with a navigation phase to a field target, and concluded with bombing runs at the NATO range at Nordhorn. Points were scored for timing and accuracy, the margin of error being timed to the second and measured by metres for the navigation exercise, and on the bombing target. Of the four sorties which achieved maximum points, three were flown by Jaguars.

In 1977, Jaguars did even better in the Salmond Trophy, taking the first four places. Each of four competing Jaguar squadrons entered 13 aircraft. No 14 was placed first for the third successive year, No 17 second, for the second successive year, No 11 (AC) third and No 31 fourth. The results were taken as confirming a statement made earlier that year by the then Chief of the Air Staff, Air Chief Marshal Sir Neil Cameron, that, 'Jaguar is 20 times as effective as the 600mph Venom of 25 years ago. We are now in "the bomb-in-a-bucket era".' During 1980, Jaguars distinguished themselves in two war exercises on the other side of the Atlantic. Six aircraft from No 20 Squadron were ferried to Goose Bay, Labrador and staged via Bagotville, North Bay and Winnipeg to the Royal Canadian Air Force base at Cold Lake to take part in Exercise Maple Flag. This was run by American staff from the USAF base at Nellis who had assembled a large armada of different types, including

RCAF CF-5Ss, CF-104s, CF-101s and C-103s. USAF F-15s and F-5Es from Nellis, acted as aggressors. In the first two weeks of the exercise No 20 pilots defied atrocious weather to fly 61 sorties, while in the second half, No 6 Squadron Jaguars, also ferried from the UK, achieved a total of 75 sorties in improved weather. The Jaguar pilots repeatedly claimed to have destroyed or damaged targets, attributing their success to the excellence of their navigation system and laser-rangers. One American colonel, after leading a less-than-successful mission was heard to coment, 'Next time we had better follow the Limeys; at least we would be able to find the target'.

Later in the year No 54 Squadron took part in Exercise Red Flag at Nellis which has a 'play pen' covering some 10m acres reserved for the practice and development of military flying. The range area within this covers three million acres and includes 50 different types of targets, including airfields, industrial complex outlines, two vehicle convoys (one of them more than 17 miles long, correctly spaced and protected by tracked anti-aircraft guns), ten miles of railway with a 10-car train, and armoured replicas of Soviet T-62 tanks deployed for battle. The targets are defended by 35 threat simulators which are similar visually, and in most cases electronically, to Soviet-built equipment.

Top: Carrying fuel tanks on the inboard wing pylons, an RAF two-seat of No 14 Squadron is flown out of Brüggen, Germany, by the station commander, Wg Cdr J. R. Walker. *BAe*

Above: Single-seater of No 31 Squadron RAF taxies in after a parachute-assisted landing pull-up. *BAe*

Early-warning radars, organised in two brigades, detect incoming aircraft at 300 miles and pass data to the Red Force filter centre at the range control centre. They in turn relay the information to Red Force brigade commanders, who order defensive operations, including the scrambling of F-5E Tiger 11s acting as interceptors, even to the extent of being camouflaged in patterns typical of Warsaw Pact aircraft. They are also flown by some of the best fighter pilots in the USAF.

No 54 Squadron pilots entered this daunting arena with some misgivings, having staged from Coltishall via Lossiemouth, Loring AFB, Rickenbacker and McConnel in two waves, but early experience indicated that the misgivings were misplaced. A stream of Jaguars armed with practice bombs launched a raid against an 'enemy' convoy 100 miles away. They flew hugging the ground at transonic speed, arrived on time

Above: Well known, but worth repeating. This pictures sums up the power of the Jaguar in the role for which it was designed — hurrying full bore for its target, low down, in murky weather. *BAe*

Left: A No 31 Squadron RAF single-seat Jaguar carrying fuel tanks and practice bomb dispensers taxies gently past an impressive array of airfield missile defences. *BAe*

without being intercepted or tracked, and saturated the target, seven aircraft streaking over it in 20 seconds. The pilots modestly put their success down to, 'a patch of European-type weather'. The real reason appeared to be that the Jaguars' small, camouflaged profiles were difficult to pick out against the desert background, while also producing a tiny signature on radar monitors which tended to merge with ground clutter, or to be missed completely.

During Red Flag, the Jaguars flew 137 sorties out of 141 planned and there was only one validated claim against one of them by fighters from the aggressor squadrons. Wg Cdr Sam Goddard, commanding officer of No 54 Squadron, summed up, 'Jaguars can take very heavy punishment, and their systems stood up to the supreme test with very few failures. Their availability was excellent throughout the exercise'. Col Gerauld Gentry, USAF commander of the Red Flag exercise, said afterwards, and one suspects somewhat ruefully, 'Our people learned a hell of a lot from the Brits.'

French Air Force Jaguars showed their competition style in May 1980, by winning both the Comète and Tactique trophies at the FAF fighter congress, held at Cazaux. A total of 31 fighter and reconnaissance squadrons participated. The Comète trophy was carried off by 3/3 Ardennes squadron, and the Tactique by 2/7 Argonne. Jaguar salesmen from British Aerospace battling in markets abroad to sell the aircraft up against Mirages did not miss the opportunity to point out that the main opponents of the successful Jaguars in the Cazaux trials were Mirages.

In August 1980, Jaguars of No 31 Squadron RAF, based at Brüggen, Germany, won both the Broadhurst Trophy for conventional bombing, and the Canberra Trophy for low-level retarded bombing in the biennial NATO tactical air meet at Ramstein. Aircraft from six other nations took part. After the RAF Jaguars had consistently laid their weapons on target within a four-second 'window', Gp Capt Ord, Assistant Chief of Staff for Offensive Operations, 2nd Allied Tactical Air Force, was heard to remark, 'If war starts tomorrow, and this is all we have, I'm happy.'

Footnote: In the summer of 1981, the RAF Jaguar front-line disposition was: two ground attack squadrons, Nos 6 and 54, and one reconnaissance squadron, No 41, at Coltishall, four strike/attack squadrons, Nos 14, 17, 20 and 31, at Brüggen, and one reconnaissance squadron No 2, at Laarbruch.

Below: A No 14 Squadron RAF single-seat Jaguar stands ready outside a hardened shelter on the airfield at Brüggen, West Germany. *RAF*

Bottom: In service. A GR Mk 1 of No 14 Squadron RAF stands outside a hardened shelter at RAF Brüggen. *BAe*

9 Selling Jaguar Abroad

From its earliest days, Jaguar had been promoted by its joint manufacturers as a potential export, but it was not until August 1974 that the first overseas sales were logged — to two countries which, BAC said at the time, 'do not wish their identities nor the quantities to be disclosed'. The buyers were in fact the Sultan of Oman's Air Force and the Ecuadorean Air Force, each of which ordered 12 at a total cost of £80million (later raised to £108million when Oman reordered a further 12).

The concept of an international version of the Jaguar was launched publicly at the Farnborough air show which was held a month later. At this event S1, the first RAF strike aircraft, which had been diverted to development was put on display as representative of the new type, together with the additional weaponry which it would be able to haul, including the Matra R550 Magic dog-fight missile carried over-wing, and the Exocet and Kormoran anti-shipping missiles, a mock-up of a new nose to contain the Agave radar, and legends indicating that there would be more powerful Adours.

Flight trials of S1, the 'prototype' Jaguar International, with uprated Adours, the Mark 804 RT172-26, and Magic missiles in the under-wing position, began in the summer of 1975. It quickly became apparent that the dash 26 would give Jaguar that extra bit of boot which had been lacking in the earlier version, providing a 27% increase in thrust at Mach 0.8/0.9 at sea level. Take-off performance was improved by 10% while there was a 30% betterment of the sustained capability which turned the aircraft into a dog-fight/air superiority machine equal to some fighters built from scratch for that job. The uprating of the engines also had the effect of improving the Jaguar's performance in hot and high conditions, a factor of obvious interest to many potential overseas customers. Dash 26 engine trials were completed by September 1975, with the new thrust ratings of 8,000lb with reheat and 5,370lb dry confirmed. The programme covered 14 flights in all, from 50,000ft down to a very low level.

Phase two of the Jaguar International concept followed, its main features being the fitting of Magics in the overwing position, and the Agave radar. These latter tests were carried out with a two-seat Jaguar and with the trial installation Agave in the nose of a 1,200-litre fuel pod beneath the fuselage. It was around this time in the development programme that King Hussein, of Jordan, flew a two-seat Jaguar, commenting afterwards, 'I am tremendously impressed by its design, and by the way it handles. I think it has a tremendous future'.

An agreement was signed with the French Thomson-CSF company for the supply of Agave. At the end of the trials, in the spring of 1977, it had been

Below: The prototype Jaguar International two-seater out on test. *BAe*

Right: Jaguar International prototype in a typical low-level strike configuration carries four 1,000lb bombs, two long-range drop tanks, and overwing Magic missiles.
BAe via Anne Tilbury

found that the addition of the radar would extend the versatility of Jaguar considerably in the air-to-sea, air-to-ground mapping and ranging, and air-to-air search and lock-on modes. Agave in the Jaguar produced detection ranges of up to 70 nautical miles against medium-sized ships and up to 15 miles against a fighter-bomber. In the trials, the radar display unit replaced the projected map display in the rear cockpit. It was decided that in the single-seat Jaguar International the radar would be fitted in the nose of the aircraft in place of the laser ranger and marked-target facilities. Information from the Agave could be displayed head-down on either a Thomson CSF display unit, or on a combined map and electronic display which superimposed the radar data over the projected map display. There was also the alternative of projecting the information on to a Smiths Raster head-up display by means of a scan converter, so obtaining the best of both systems, and the retention of the existing projected map display.

Purchasers who wished to retain the laser ranger and marked-target facilities, and thus avoid loss of range accuracy when carrying out very low-level laydown bomb attacks over undulating ground, were offered the alternative of a smaller Ferranti 105S laser-ranging system fitted into a small chin fairing behind the Agave radar nose. The first custom-built Jaguar International (G27-266) flew for the first time on 19 August 1976. Deliveries to Ecuador began in January 1977, and were completed by October; to Oman they began in the March and were completed in the spring of 1978, although Oman reordered later. Oman was one of the places of call for a two-seat Jaguar fitted with dash 26 engines which beat the International version drum in a sales tour around the Middle East in late 1975. Flown from Warton by Peter Ginger, BAC military aircraft division's chief production test pilot, and navigator Roy Kenward, the aircraft also visited Abu Dhabi, Dubai, Saudi Arabia, Qatar, Kuwait, Tehran and Turkey. Although BAC said after the 15,000-mile, six-week demonstration, that, 'tremendous interest' had been shown by air forces, nobody else in that area placed orders.

Below: This Jaguar International single-seat is festooned with Magic missiles overwing, six cluster bombs on the underwing stations, and 264gal fuel tank beneath the fuselage. *BAe*

The calibre of the aircraft, and the confidence of its crews in it was illustrated by the decision to carry out flight deliveries (in contrast to the practice of shipping adopted for all Mirages to Latin America) without support aircraft or any engineering assistance en route. The aircraft were staged in pairs via West Africa, Ascension and Brazil, thereafter crossing the northern part of the continent to their destination. The merits of the navigation system were evident particularly on the long over-water Atlantic leg of 1,224 nautical miles from Ascension to Recife without updating on fixes. System errors were noted to be small on arrival.

The Indian government announced its choice of Jaguar International over the French Mirage F1 and the Swedish Viggen in October 1978. An official statement from Delhi said:

'For some time the Indian Air Force has felt the need for replacing its ageing and obsolescent fleet of Canberras and Hunters, which have been in service since the 1950s, and which are at present being phased out. This has entailed an evaluation of all available aircraft which would adequately fulfil the requirements of the IAF. At an early stage of consideration it was decided that the aircraft to be selected, apart from meeting the requirements of the air force, would also be one which could as speedily as possible be produced within the country.

'Therefore, two objectives were borne in mind; one, what was the best from the defence angle and, two, the need for self-reliance. Having regard to these objectives, the field of choice was narrowed to three aircraft, namely the Jaguar, the Mirage F1 and the Viggen. The relative merits of these aircraft were evaluated at the professional level in all their aspects. Detailed negotiations were also conducted with the manufacturers in respect of such matters as prices, delivery schedules, and transfer of technology for organising indigenous production.

'Based on this evaluation and these negotiations, it has now been decided that the aircraft which will replace the fleet of Canberras and Hunters will be the Jaguar. Firstly, the Jaguar — as also the other two aircraft — adequately meets the requirements of the IAF. Secondly, it is the most economical of the three options. Thirdly, it has the most favourable delivery schedule. Fourthly, the Jaguar has an edge over the other two aircraft in the important characteristic of survival capability, being the only twin-engine aircraft of the three.'

The Indians made it clear at this time that an important feature of the contract for them would be that almost three quarters of the projected requirements of the aircraft would be produced in their

Above: Jaguar International B01 was the first two-seat version in desert camouflage for the Sultan of Oman's Air Force. It is seen here on a test flight, and taking off from the airfield at Warton. *BAe*

country. There would also be a buy-back arrangement of items manufacture in India.

The intention to proceed (ITP) was signed between the Indians and British Aerospace in Delhi at the end of October, 1978, covering both fly-away aircraft to be bought initially from Britain, and licensed manufacture. The signing gave BAes the green light to manufacture the first few aircraft, for Hindustan Aeronautics, the Indian manufacturer, to begin establishing a Jaguar production line, and for the IAF to initiate the training of pilots and ground crew. India had contracted to buy an initial 40 aircraft and to make a further 120, the whole deal being said to be worth up to £1,000m.

The deal was soon under fire in the Indian Parliament and was defended by the Defence Minister, Mr Jagjivan Ram. He said that the procurement decision had not been taken by his ministry alone, but by the Cabinet political affairs committee, and without any intermediary being involved. The Jaguar was definitely cheaper than the F1, and its package included equipment, weapons, spares, modifications, safety items, technical assistance, licence fees and royalties. Cost evaluations had been taken at all levels. Jaguar production with British collaboration would begin in 1982-83, and one of the main features of the agreement would be the sharing of any future technological improvement in the Adour engine by the manufacturers. Hindustan Aeronautics would concentrate airframe and engine work in Bangalore, with accessory manufacture at Lucknow and Hyderabad.

Mr James Ascroft, deputy chief experimental engineer of British Aerospace, visited HAL at Bangalore and said he was satisfied that the technical force available could be geared for Jaguar production after training in the UK, and that HAL had the capability to undertake licensed manufacture. He was satisfied with the production techniques and quality control in HAL, but it would be necessary to update technology by about ten years. About 40 engineers from the UK would be with HAL for a year or two to launch production of the Jaguar, and the first Indian-assembled version was due to be rolled out in mid-1982. About 50 would be assembled mainly from British-built sub-assemblies before an increasing pro-

Above: Jaguar Internationals of the Omani Air Force in their hangar at Thumrait, built as part of that country's integrated air defence system. *BAe*

portion to Indian components was introduced. Production from raw materials was expected to result in the first HAL-built Jaguar appearing in 1984.

The first four officers from IAF chosen to fly the Jaguar arrived at 226 OCU, RAF Lossiemouth on 26 February 1979, when they joined four British pilots, a Dane, and a West German on course No 29. The IAF men took to their new aircraft without any great problems, not surprisingly, as they had between them had experience of 36 different types, including the Su-7, MiG-21, Draken, Viggen, F-104 and Hawk, and were combat veterans. The first IAF officer/NCO ground support technician course assembled at Warton on the same day, splitting into six specialist groups covering airframe, engines, electrics, avionics, radar, and an officers' course which included all the engineering aspects. At the end of the course, some members dispersed to various vendor factories in the UK to see construction and final assembly procedures at first hand, while others remained at Warton for further study.

Handing-over of the first two interim Jaguars for the IAF took place at a formal ceremony at Warton on 19 July 1979, with Dr I. P. Singh, the Acting High Commissioner for India in the UK, receiving them from Sir Frederick Page, Chairman and chief executive of the BAe aircraft group. The aircraft were refurbished RAF machines, eventually to be returned, a B version two-seat and an S version single-seat. They were flown out to India as a pair, arriving on 27 July. The B was piloted by Tim Ferguson, deputy chief test pilot of the Warton division, with Wg Cdr D. R. Nadkarni, officer commanding designate of the first IAF Jaguar squadron, in the second seat, and the S by Chris Yeo, BAe's Jaguar project test pilot. The second pair of IAF Jaguars arrived in India on 14 October that year. Once again they consisted of a B and an S, but on this occasion Wg Cdr Nadkarni flew the B, with Paul Millett, executive director of flight operations at Warton, accompanying him, while the S was piloted by Sqn Ldr M. McMahon IAF. In July 1980, 'Mike' McMahon, by this time promoted to wing commander, took the Indian Minister of State for Defence, Mr C. P. N. Singh, for a demonstration ride in an IAF Jaguar. They took off from Palam airport, Delhi, and covered a large part of the Himalayan region during a 35-minute flight, most of it at Mach 1.1 at 18,000ft. On landing, the minister, according to BAe, was 'obviously delighted' and commented favourably on the light controls and the available power.

By this juncture in the Indian Jaguar deal, the British company needed all the friends in high places on the sub-continent it could get. In his speech in July the previous year at the formal handing over of the first two aircraft, Sir Frederick Page had expressed his thanks to the French companies involved in the project for its success, but by 1980 the French, although full partners in Jaguar, were snapping at the heels of BAe and trying to have the Indian deal cancelled in favour of their indigenous fighter aircraft.

According to reports from Delhi, the French ambassador there had gone to the Defence Ministry on the day before the intention to purchase had been signed with BAe and to offer to buy the deal out, and to supply F1s from the French Air Force as an interim step towards India taking a fleet of Mirage 2000s. The offer was repeated in January 1980 by the French President Giscard d'Estaing when he met the Indian Prime Minister, Mrs Gandhi, reminding her that the Jaguar order had been negotiated and placed by the rival Janata government, which her party had recently put out of office. At the time of writing, the Indians had not acceded to the French blandishments, although there was obvious interest within some sections of the government in Delhi in truncating the Jaguar deal. France and India were fast becoming major trading partners, but this French advantage was

Left: The Himalayan mountains provide a dramatic backdrop for this Indian Air Force Jaguar.
Image in Industry

Above: The first two Jaguars for the Indian Air Force. Top is a two-seat being flown by Tim Ferguson, British Aerospace test pilot, and Wg Cdr D. R. Nadkarni, of the IAF, who completed the Jaguar operational conversion course in the UK, and who was commander designate of the first IAF Jaguar squadron. The lower aircraft is a single-seat S version being flown by Chris Yeo, Jaguar project test pilot.
BAe

Right: Wg Cdr D. R. Nadkarni (left) and Air Marshal Dilbagh Singh of the Indian Air Force pose in front of the first IAF two-seat after its delivery flight from the UK. *BAe*

overridden by the fact that the Jaguar existed and was in service in large numbers, whereas the 2000 was not due to go into production until 1985.

Other burdens borne by the French aircraft against the Jaguar included, that it would cost some 50% more than the Jaguar, that its purchase would increase still further the share of defence funds won by the IAF, and which many considered to be already disproportionately high, and that the Pakistan Air Force, India's old adversary in three wars in 20 years, looked as if it would buy the French aircraft type. The ritual dancing in the corridors of power of Delhi was watched closely from Warton, where jobs were at stake. In a trenchant leading article, the local newspaper, the *Evening Post* considered the French efforts to sabotage the Jaguar deal as, 'positively malevolent', and recorded that the local MP, Mr Edward Gardner, had suggested that the word for the French machinations was, 'Machiavellian'. And in a second leader on the same subject, the same journal commented, 'The contract is of importance to British Aerospace at Warton; changes now will make nonsense of international agreements, and will not heighten job prospects in our aviation industry, which has had more than its share of the effects of political wranglings since the war'. And the paper added, darkly, 'We should not forget the origins of M Chauvin'. But while such doubts were being raised at the political level, the IAF got steadily on with the task of putting its new aircraft into service. By the summer of 1980, the first IAF squadron had reported itself fully operational, and by September of that same year the first batch of aircraft under the ITP signed two years previously had been completed and delivered from the Warton factory.

Below: Four Jaguars destined for the Fuerza Aerea Ecuadoriana. Ecuador was the second international customer for the aircraft, after Oman. *BAe*

10 Now Try to Stop it!

'Pick your target, specify your defences — now just try to stop a well-flown Jaguar.' So concluded one RAF Jaguar pilot in a graphic description of just what it is like to fly the aircraft. He said:

'*Panthera onca* is reputed to be the fiercest of the big cats. Its aeronautical namesake, the Jaguar . . . is likely to demonstrate all the qualities of the feline which cause its prey to fear it most.

'It is designed for, and excels at, the aggressive role of strike/attack at very high speeds and at very low levels. As a single-seater in the most demanding role of all, it offers the pilot a unique challenge, for never before has the Service operated an aircraft with such speed, payload, range and flexibility of attack options, and offered the package to one man. Those who accept the challenge are rewarded with the most exciting flying available today, and wear the triangular Jaguar patch with justifiable pride.

'Walking out to the aircraft to fly a typical training mission, the first impression is that the Jaguar is a big aircraft. This is quite a false impression because the Jaguar is only about the same size as a Hunter, and considerably smaller than the Phantom or Buccaneer. The impression of size is given by the undercarriage legs which sit the aircraft very much higher on the ground than one expects of aircraft of this size. The undercarriage, a most forgiving friend of the pilot, has clearly been designed with operations from semi-prepared surfaces or damaged runways in mind.

'Before inspecting the aircraft the first task is to start the alignment of the navigation and weapon aiming sub system (NAVWASS). This exotic name refers to a series of "black boxes" producing navigation and weapon-aiming information. Together, this information gives the single pilot the capability to accomplish results which in the past have taken crews to achieve. It is based on a digital computer, and magical though its powers may be, as with all computers, it is not intelligent. The pilot first has to tell the NAVWASS where it is in latitude and longitude, and its height above sea level, after which it can "align" itself and thereafter produce navigational and weapon-aiming solutions from inertially sensing the aircraft's movement about three principal axes. The process of initiating the alignment takes only a few seconds.

'Checking around the outside of the aircraft, two features stand out. First, the wings are very small and very thin. This indicates that the aircraft is designed for flight at high transonic and supersonic Mach numbers. The outboard sections of the trailing edge masquerade as ailerons, but are part of the trailing edge flaps which on this wing are full-span. These are

Below: S07, the second Jaguar to be produced to RAF specification, carries four 1,170lb retarded bombs, two on each inner wing pylon, two Matra 155 rocket launchers, each containing 18 SNEB rockets, on the outer pylons, and a 264gal fuel tank on the under-fuselage pylon. The weaponry weighed 9,000lb, 1,000lb below the maximum load. S07 was rolled out on 25 March 1970. *BAe*

Above: Eight practice bomb carriers are clipped under the wings and body of two-seat B1, seen on the airfield at Warton. *BAe*

complemented by nearly full span slats on the leading edge and, with both deployed, the decidedly supersonic wing takes on an encouraging subsonic camber, and allows the aircraft to land slower than most of its contemporaries. The second major feature is at the back, where the size of the exhaust pipes of the two Adour engines excites some comment, particularly from pilots fresh off other fighters such as Phantom, Buccaneer and Lightning, aircraft whose jet pipes have cavernous appearance. It is the economy of these fan engines that is largely responsible for the impressive range of the aircraft.

'The cockpit layout is excellent, with flight instruments to the left, and engine and fuel controls and indicators to the right of the central strip of the NAVWASS equipment. At the top there is the head-up display (HUD) which gives the pilot all the information he needs to fly the aircraft, navigate to the target, and deliver his weapons. Underneath this is a control panel to vary the comprehensive information available for display in the HUD (eg airspeed or Mach no, barometric or radar height, flight director, and incidence information, etc).

'In the central position below the HUD is situated the projected map display (PMD), or "moving" map. To a newcomer to modern navigation systems, the moving map is the outward manifestation of the wizardry contained in the black boxes. As with the HUD, the map also allows a variety of options, including a look-ahead facility where the target or turning point (waypoint) can be selected and studied with the map, either north or track orientated or, as more usually, with the present position of the aircraft shown in the centre of the map, again with the option of north or track orientation. The map scale itself can be changed between approximately 1:500,000 and 1:250,000 scale, which gives great flexibility.

'Immediately above and to the left is the horizontal situation indicator (HSI) control. This controls another range of options varying between "direct" information from aids such as TACAN, or computer modes with the choice of true or magnetic heading information.

'Shutting the canopy (manually controlled, rubber bungee counter-balanced, easy to maintain, and reliable) reveals an excellent view, particularly to the rear. The view to the low front is equally good, and this is increasingly important when the sighting of modern, retarded weapons is considered. Starting the engines is straightforward, and the aircraft taxies at all but very high weights at idle power. It is during taxiing that the pilot immediately feels at home in the aircraft. The undercarriage is soft and compliant and gives a very smooth ride, the nosewheel steering is positive, and the brakes are powerful. At slow speeds, the aircraft turns in its own length and, with such a narrow span, small manoeuvring areas can be used safely.

'Take-off is always made in reheat. Lift-off speed comes quickly, and undercarriage and flaps need to be retracted without undue delay if the limiting speeds are not to be exceeded. By the end of the runway, speed is

Left: Another hardware display of stores in the Jaguar inventory, showing the range of permutations which the armourers have within a total uplift of 10,000lb. *BAe*

Below: The choice of lethal hardware for Jaguar was laid out at the 1978 Farnborough show, but the radar nose is discreetly covered over. *Brian M. Service*

approaching the 300kts mark, at which point the engines are throttled back out of reheat. Acceleration is continued in dry power to the route speed, which is usually in the region of 450kts.

'Before take-off, the NAVWASS is selected to the first waypoint so, by the time the normal after-take-off checks have been made, the system is anxious that the pilot obeys the many instructions he is now being given. Head-up, the heading indicators may be giving a direction to fly left or right and up and down, depending on which "demanded height" has been used to capture the track to the target. Head-down, the moving map will show present track and direction to steer to the waypoint. The HSI will be showing track, heading to steer, the distance to go to the waypoint, drift, and how far off track the aircraft may be.

'The unwary could become confused at this point because the NAVWASS may be demanding a turn when the pilot knows full well he is on the correct heading for the waypoint following take-off. In this case, the HSI will be showing that, perhaps because of runway direction of departure patterns, the aircraft, although heading for the waypoint, may be to the right or left of a track drawn directly from the airfield to the waypoint. The turn demand is therefore an attempt to get the aircraft back on the direct or designated track. This will be achieved by programmed turns giving acceptable capture angles. If, however, the pilot elects not to regain the direct track, he may "change destination" at that (or any other) point, and the computer will calculate a track direct from the present position to the waypoint, and the map, HUD and HSI will show the aircraft on track.

'The tactical implications of this facility are important. A track may be planned under operational conditions to transit between known defended sites, or to take advantage of natural terrain cover, associated operations, etc. In this case, although a diversion from the original track may be necessary for weather or enemy interference, the return to the originally-planned track can be made with ease and assurance. Under high workload conditions, this facility is most important, and allows the pilot greater freedom of action than ever before.

'Another advantage is in the planning of a mission where quick reaction argues for brief planning. In Jaguar, only the waypoints need to be plotted — the turns can be either allowed for by letting the NAVWASS steer the aircraft back on to the direct track between the waypoints or, alternatively, a press of the "change destination" button on completion of the turn will designate a new track from that point direct to the waypoint.

'Time on target (TOT) has always been an important factor in strike/attack operations for, in modern warfare, the difficulties of integrating widely differing forces in a battle area may require time separation. The lifting of an artillery attack to allow aircraft to conduct their attack, or the lifting of a ground-based air defence alert to allow aircraft to penetrate our own defensive lines en route to and from deep targets, are but two examples of a need for most

Left: Lossiemouth shows its Jaguar teeth, and the squadron mascot gets pride of place.
Harry Kerr, The Times

Right: Armament options for Jaguar are laid out on display at the Farnborough air show.
Harry Kerr, The Times

accurate timings in ground attack operations. High accuracies have been achieved in the past, and such accuracies will not be new to the Jaguar force. What will be new is the ease with which those accuracies can now be achieved.

'The most important factor in holding a time schedule is the ability to fly at the ground-speed used in calculating the total route time. In Jaguar, once settled into the initial part of the sortie, a selection on the NAVWASS will cause ground speed to be displayed on opticators in the cockpit. Airspeed is increased or decreased until this reading gives the planned ground speed, then the sortie is flown on the HUD indicated airspeed corresponding to the desired ground speed. This system prevents gross errors building up, and TOTs within seconds will consistently be achieved. Height can be read in digital form from the HUD off the radar altimeter or as a barometric response. For many pilots, this is the first time height information of such accuracy has been available to them. This gives the operational benefits that, when position of enemy defences is known, the aircraft can be flown with confidence below the effective engagement levels of the enemy equipment. [Later programmes used by the RAF incorporate a demanded groundspeed facility. The desired time on target is set into the computer, which then calculates the groundspeed required to make that time; the pilot then matches his actual groundspeed to the demanded groundspeed, and 'hey presto'.]

Left: View from the rear cockpit of a two-seat Jaguar on its take-off run catches the lead aircraft a split second after lifting off. *Image in Industry.*

Below left: Not just a pretty trainer. A Jaguar two-seat roars off the ground at the BAC airfield at Warton loaded with four 1,000lb bombs and a 1,200-litre fuel tank on the centreline. *BAe*

Right and below: Trials from a motorway near Blackpool, England, proved Jaguar's capability to operate away from prepared runways in times of conflict. Piloted by Tim Ferguson, BAC's military division deputy chief test pilot, the GR Mk 1 aircraft starts its taxi run under a motorway bridge, to the evident pain of onlookers, lifts off alongside the central crash barrier, and then lands and uses the tail 'chute to make a short pull-up. *BAe*

'Once stabilised at high speed and at low level, the truly-excellent handling qualities of the aircraft come to the fore. Turbulence is ironed out particularly well, and even on rough days speed does not have to be reduced. The aircraft will give the lie to many armchair critics who regularly pontificate how fast and low a pilot can fly. Because more time can be spent looking out of the cockpit, the first indication of approaching the waypoint may be the change in the HUD symbols. A "time-to-go" circle will appear at 70 seconds to go to the waypoint, and a cross will indicate the computed position of the turning point. The circle remains complete until one minute to go, and then winds down counter clockwise. On sighting the turning point, the next waypoint or the target can be selected, and on "changing destination", the navigational process continues as before.

'The leg to the target will be flown in the same manner, and the NAVWASS will enter the close navigation phase indicated by the "time-to-go" circle, or the target acquisition mode, depending on which has been selected. The pilot then decides which of the many and flexible attack options he wishes to adopt. The first decision will be to select the weapon to be used, and here the additional flexibility of five pylons

Above: Jaguar demonstrates its effectiveness against armour in a test against tank targets on a range in Scotland. The aircraft is dropping two 600lb Hunting Engineering BL755 cluster bombs, each of which spring open to release around 290 bomblets, straddling completely the targets.
Image in Industry

becomes apparent, three of which can carry stores in tandem. When stores are loaded, the computer is told which store is loaded on which pylon. The correct ballistics are fed into the equations but, most important, the computer logic refuses to accept non-valid instructions from the pilot resulting in a weapon delivery sight picture not being obtainable. This alone is normally sufficient to make the pilot realise his error, and reselect the correct mode.

'The next decision is whether to make a semi-automatic or an automatic attack. In the former, the actual release pulse is generated by the pilot after positioning a bomb-fall line on the target, and awaiting the target and the continuously-computed impact point to become coincident. In automatic attacks, the pilot positions a ground-stabilised bar on the target and, when this and the continuously-computed impact point become coincident, the weapons are released automatically. The advantages of the automatic release modes are that target position is indicated in the HUD and so aids target acquisition, and that indications of safe delivery parameters are available, so reducing the danger of self-damage from bomb fragmentation. A completely-manual attack mode is also available to Jaguar pilots.

'Immediately the weapons are released, the HUD reverts to a navigational mode and directs the pilot to the next target, waypoint or rendezvous area. Throughout the escape phase, the pilot can concentrate entirely on evasion and pick up the navigation again when the situation allows. Flying in sections of Jaguars poses problems, for the aircraft is small, and in head-on or tail-on aspects presents a very fine profile. This, allied to excellent camouflaging, makes it difficult to keep in contact when flying in battle formation. Intercept pilots find it particularly difficult to acquire visually.

'Perhaps at the end of an attack training mission, the time and fuel will be available to take the aircraft out of its design environment of low level and take it to high level. This is far more of an exhilarating experience than the uninitiated would expect. For a primarily low-level attack aircraft, the pull-out from low level, reheat climb to the tropopause, acceleration to a substantial supersonic speed, zoom climb to 45,000ft, and then tactical descent to sea level, all within five minutes, prove that nations looking for a secondary air defence capability may, with the addition of comparatively cheap missiles, have quite an impressive capability.

'In the circuit the aircraft is flown with half flap, which also activates the leading-edge slat. This allows circuits to be flown at speeds very low for a high-performance aircraft. With full flap on finals, relatively high-power settings are required, but no more so than with aircraft of comparable performance. Handling and response in the circuit pattern are at all times positive. The aircraft is easy to land, and with the compliant undercarriage, the actual touchdowns are soft and smooth.

'The runway performance on landing is another of the impressive features of the aircraft. With fat tyres, big brakes, nose-wheel steering and a huge braking parachute, the stopping distance is remarkably short. This facility for dissipating energy allows the single-

Left: On a practice pass over the sea at 300ft and 450kts, Jaguar S07 releases a 1,000lb retarded bomb. This was part of the trials of the navigation and weapon aiming system which produced high accuracies from the earliest days. *BAe*

Below: In this hardware configuration, Jaguar S07 carries two 1,000lb bombs under its fuselage, and a 1,200-litre fuel tank beneath each wing. This air-to-air picture, dated January, 1971, was the first to be released showing a British Jaguar carrying external stores. *BAe*

engine myth to be finally laid to rest. In early development aircraft with pre-production engines, the Jaguar picked up a reputation for poor performances on one engine. The technique being taught in the RAF makes it one of the safest aircraft on one engine to enter service. Speed can safely be maintained, sufficient to overshoot from touchdown if necessary, and recourse made to the multitude of stopping aids to complete the landing safely. If all else fails — and it would take double, if not triple failure to cause it to do so — the emergency hook can take the wire of the emergency arrester gear. [The early single-engine approach difficulties mentioned here were eradicated as part of a development programme by the engine and airframe manufacturers, so that the aircraft can today be both flown and landed satisfactorily on one engine using part-throttle reheat.]

'The Jaguar has acquired a reputation among its pilots in the RAF as a potent weapon . . . It is a pilot's aeroplane, and each sortie is a rewarding experience. It seems that every so often the world's aircraft industry produces a really "good one" — Canberra from the late 1940s, Hunter in the early 1950s, Phantom from the other side of the Atlantic. Jaguar will rate alongside these in the affections of its pilots. For those who still doubt, a gauntlet: Pick your own target, specify your defences; now just try to stop a well-flown Jaguar.'

Appendix: Jaguar Attrition

Date	*Serial*	*Model*	*Unit*	*Operator*	*Location*	*Remarks*
26/3/70	E-O1	E	CEAM	France AF	Istres, France	1st Prototype. Crashed on approach after fire in No 2 engine. Total time 130 hours approx.
14/2/72	A-O3	A	CEAM	French AF	Tarnos, France	Written-off as result of heavy landing.
11/8/72	XW560	GR1	A & AEE	MoD	Boscombe Down, UK	Burnt out in ground fire.
22/11/74	XX136	T2	A & AEE	MoD	Wimborne St Giles, UK	
25/3/75	E-26	E	—	SEPECAT	16 miles NE of Reims, France	Crashed on pre-delivery test flight.
30/4/75	XX831	T2	226 OCU	RAF	Lossiemouth,UK	
6/2/76	XX137	T2	226 OCU	RAF	Lossiemouth, UK	Crashed into Moray Firth. Ran out of fuel following leak in low pressure system.
2/7/76	XX822	GR1	14 Sqn	RAF	15 miles W of Alhorn, FRG	Pilot killed. First fatality.
15/9/76	XX735	GR1	6 Sqn	RAF	Eggebek, FRG	Crashed during Exercise 'Teamwork '76'.
17/9/76	XX120	GR1	54 Sqn	RAF	Samsoe Island, Denmark	Crashed into sea during Exercise 'Teamwork '76'.
14/12/76	XZ102	GR1	2 Sqn	RAF	10 miles NE of Laarbruch, FRG	
14/1/77	?	A	11^e Esc	French AF	Villers-sous-Preny, France	Pilot ejected safely.
14/2/77	A-18	A	7^e Esc	French AF	Troyes, France	
25/2/77	XZ120	GR1	2 Sqn	RAF	Nordholm, Denmark	Crashed into North Sea.
14/6/77	XX978	GR1	31 Sqn	RAF	Verden, FRG	Crashed into a house. Pilot killed.
29/7/77	XX148	T2	226 OCU	RAF	Whittingham, UK	Crew killed.
12/77	?	A	11^e Esc	French AF	Mauritania	Shot down by Polisario guerillas near border with Chad
12/77	?	A	11^e Esc	French AF	Mauritania	Shot down by Polisario guerillas. Second lost to ground fire during month.
21/3/78	XX971	GR1	31 Sqn	RAF	Lahr, FRG	Crashed on take-off during exchange visit with RCAF.
27/4/78	XX149	T2	226 OCU	RAF	Cullen, Banff, UK	Flew into mountain.
3/5/78	?	A	11^e Esc	French AF	Mauritania	Shot down by Polisario guerillas.
31/5/78	?	A	11^e Esc	French AF	Chad	
6/6/78	XX761	GR1	226 OCU	RAF	Lossiemouth, UK	Ground fire. Cockpit section salvaged and allocated to ground instruction as 8600M.

Date	*Serial*	*Model*	*Unit*	*Operator*	*Location*	*Remarks*
25/7/78	XX823	GR1	17 Sqn	RAF	Cagliari, Sardinia	Flew into hill during armament practice sortie while on detachment to Decimomannu.
8/8/78	?	A	11^e^ Esc	French AF	Ati, Chad	Crashed on reconnaissance flight.
23/8/78	?	A	11^e^ Esc	French AF	400kms from Ndjamena, Chad	Crashed after collision with another Jaguar. Second aircraft returned to base safely.
14/10/78	—	A	11^e^ Esc	French AF	Ndjamena, Chad	
1/11/78	XX759	GR1	226 OCU	RAF	Selkirk, UK	Ecuadorean pilot killed.
26/2/79	212	S(O)1	8 Sqn	SOAF	Oman	
26/3/79	XX147	T2	17 Sqn	RAF	Sudlohn, FRG	Bird strike. Crew ejected safely.
20/6/79	A-62	A	3^e^ Esc	Franch AF	Nancy-Ochey, France	Pilot killed.
22/6/79	XX142	T2	226 OCU	RAF	10 miles from Lossiemouth, UK	Crashed into Moray Firth.
12/7/79	A-45	A	7^e^ Esc	RAF	Norvenich, FRG	Pilot ejected safely.
17/7/79	?	A	?	French AF	Siegenburg, FRG	Pilot ejected safely.
18/7/79	XX960	GR1	14 Sqn	RAF	Iserlohn, FRG	Pilot ejected safely.
23/11/79	XX762	GR1	226 OCU	RAF	Near Dalmally, Argyll, UK	Crashed into mountains.
10/12/79	XX749	GR1	226 OCU	RAF	Lumsden, Aberdeenshire, UK	Collided with XX755 while flying low-level training exercise. One pilot killed.
10/12/79	XX755	GR1	226 OCU	RAF	Lumsden, Aberdeenshire, UK	Collided with XX749; as above.
28/5/80	XX961	GR1	17 Sqn	RAF	Bruggen, FRG	Collided with XX964 overhead airfield during landing break. One pilot killed.
28/5/80	XX964	GR1	17 Sqn	RAF	Bruggen, FRG	Collided with XX961; see above.
17/7/80	XX817	GR1	17 Sqn	RAF	Munchen Gladbach, FRG	Pilot ejected.
2/81	?	A	3^e^ Esc	French AF	Nancy-Ochey, France	Squadron commander killed.
12/2/81	XX827	GR1	31 Sqn	RAF	Nellis Ranges, Nevada, USA	Crashed during 'Red Flag' exercises.
1/3/81	201	B(O)2	8 Sqn	SOAF	22 miles N of Thumrayt, Oman	Crew ejected safely.
18/3/81	?	A	11^e^ Esc	French AF	14km N of Toul, France	
14/4/81	XX973	GR1	31 Sqn	RAF	4 miles NW of Gutersloh, FRG	
1/6/81	?	T2	226 OCU	RAF	Near Kurriemuir, UK	
17/7/81	?	GR1	226 OCU	RAF	Malvern, UK	Pilot ejected.
24/7/81	?	T2	ETPS	MoD	12 miles from Hartland Point, UK	Crashed into sea.

Notes

1) **The above list may not represent a complete record of Jaguar attrition, especially in respect of French aircraft. All losses known by 29/7/81 are included.**
2) **The following French Air Force aircraft are known to have been written-off, and probably correspond to some of the unidentified aircraft above: A-52, A-71, A-106, A-109 and A-111.**

Below: Pilot walk-round. One of the first Jaguars to be delivered to the RAF comes in for close inspection on the RAF station at Lossiemouth, Scotland.
Harry Kerr, The Times